MW01273866

SEMINARS TO
BUILD YOUR BUSINESS

Barbara Siskind

Self-Counsel Press
(a division of)
International Self-Counsel Press Ltd.
U.S.A.   Canada

Copyright © 1998 by International Self-Counsel Press Ltd.

All rights reserved.

Purchasers are authorized to reproduce checklists or samples from this book without prior written permission, providing reproduction is for personal use only and does not constitute republication of this book in any form. Inquiries should be addressed to International Self-Counsel Press Ltd.

No other part of this book may be reproduced or transmitted in any form by any means — graphic, electronic, or mechanical — without permission in writing from the publisher, except by a reviewer who may quote brief passages in a review.

Self-Counsel Press acknowledges the financial support of the Government of Canada through the Book Publishing Industry Development Program for our publishing activities.

Printed in Canada.

First edition: April 1998

Canadian Cataloguing in Publication Data
    Siskind, Barbara.
    Seminars to build your business

    (Self-counsel business series)
    ISBN 1-55180-176-0

    1. Seminars — Handbooks, manuals, etc.
2. Communication in management. I. Title. II. Series.
HF5734.5S57 1998   658.4'56   C98-910254-8

Figures #1 – #9 reproduced by permission.

Self-Counsel Press
(a division of)
International Self-Counsel Press Ltd.

1704 N. State Street	1481 Charlotte Road
Bellingham, WA 98225	North Vancouver, BC V7J 1H1
U.S.A.	Canada

To the person who has been encouraging me to write this book for several years: Barry Siskind, my wonderful, passionate, sexy, romantic, supportive, patient husband. I finally listened. Without your inspiration and prodding, this book would have never happened. Thanks.

CONTENTS

SAMPLES

FIGURES

ACKNOWLEDGMENTS

When I began this project, I had concerns. My husband had written books before and told me that writing a business book requires the support of a lot of people to help, advise, and cheer me on. He was right, and so to all of you were there for me, thank you.

Special thanks to the many people who shared their seminar experiences with me, particularly, Raymond Aaron of the Raymond Aaron Group; Rena Amer of Add Value International; Dr. Calvin Breslin of Laser Sight Centre; Mark Carriere of Carriage Hills Resort; Travina Chong of Holiday Inn on King, Toronto; David Disher of Canadian Airlines International; Judy Grant of the Pacific Fertility Centre; Tom Johnson of the Tom Johnson Marketing Group; Elizabeth Lewis of the Canadian Direct Mail Association; Kelly Mac-Donald of the David Lavin Agency; Chris McDowall of CHFI, Toronto; Mary Mursell of Senior Tours Canada; Lisa Nymark of the International Snoring Association; Harry Plack of Harry Plack Associates; Tony Pillard of the Hotel Association of Canada; Cathy Reed of International Teledata Group; Alison Roberts of Canadian Crossroads International; Tracey Marshall of Security Financial Services and Investment Corporation; Pam and David Stern of Stern Auto Collision; and Marlene White of Lifestyle Retirement Communities.

Ken Mark was so helpful in my original edit and flexible in working to a very tight schedule.

Thanks also to my children Mark Silverberg and Linda Ceresne who helped me with some of the background information.

To my other children Robert and Cory Silverberg and Geoffrey and Jillian Siskind: I know that you have always been supportive of me, but I'm not sure you really understood what it is that I do. Maybe now you will know.

1
USING SEMINARS TO
PROSPECT FOR BUSINESS

a. WHY SEMINARS?

Seminars are persuasive presentations that provide an exchange of information. Persuasive — that's the key word. In every case, whether the organization or individual considering the seminar is looking for sales, recruits, donations, or community action, persuasion is the key to success.

Today, more people than ever before are using prospecting seminars to help "grow their businesses." You are probably familiar with the seminars offered by financial and real estate firms offering seminars with titles such as "Buy Real Estate with Nothing Down," "The Secrets of Getting Rich Slowly," and "Learn the Secrets of the Super Rich." But seminar marketing is not limited to these types of businesses: there is a seminar application for almost any business. You will find in Appendix 1 detailed examples of how both large and small companies have used seminars successfully to find new business.

Increasingly, businesses are using seminars as another tool to market their products or services. Seminars are part of the marketing investment in the overall business plan. These types of seminars are *not* profit centers; your objective in running prospecting seminars should be the payoff *after* the event. In chapter 2 you will learn how to develop the objectives that will bring real rewards.

Your actual out-of-pocket expenses for running a marketing seminar can range anywhere from $500 to more than

$15,000, depending on the sophistication of your program. In Appendix 1, you can read about seminars that fall into both ends of the scale.

Seminars are different from traditional marketing tools such as television, radio, and print advertising; brochures; direct mail; fax broadcast; trade shows; and referrals. If you run your business well, you have learned that each marketing tool has its advantages and disadvantages. You also know the value of marketing and understand that business competition is increasing as innovative products and services become readily available to serve the consumer.

What does this mean for you? It means you need to update the tools you use to build your business and ensure future growth. More and more, marketing involves creating new and innovative ways of reaching your audience, and one effective tool that many businesses are turning to is the prospecting seminar, which provides an excellent method of showing off your expertise while providing participants with new ideas on how to improve the quality of their lives and the productivity of their businesses.

While these same objectives can be accomplished by other marketing methods, prospecting seminars offer the advantage of face-to-face contact. At a seminar, people have an opportunity to learn about new products and services; by seeing and talking to you, they are able to arrive at more informed buying decisions. They also have opportunities to find partners with whom they can do business.

Recently, I attended a seminar hosted by a financial institution. It had invited some of its portfolio managers to host a round-table discussion for an audience of investors. I sat at the back and observed the interaction between the panel and the audience. What struck me was that there was no information given at this seminar that was not available in other forms — annual statements, newspaper articles, and

2

the company's Web site. So why was the room filled to capacity?

That answer confirms the premise for holding the seminar in the first place. People attend seminars for an opportunity to hear the information directly from the horse's mouth. In this case, as the speakers in turn explained their views, we in the audience received different perspectives on the same problem. The audience was able to take otherwise dry information and watch it come to life. Presenters were able to convey their individual passions to the audience, and the audience was able to share in that enthusiasm.

If you want to build your business, you need to share your experiences. Letting your prospective customers live and breathe the solutions you have to offer is an excellent way to get them involved. The more they can share the experience, the stronger their desire to do business with you.

At a prospecting seminar, participants learn new information presented in an entertaining and informative package, while at the same time having opportunities to interact with experts who can help them bridge the gap between abstract theory and specific use. Most marketing tools are cold and impersonal. But seminars, because they involve people, are just the opposite: they are warm and personal. Seminars provide participants an opportunity to get away from their computers, televisions, and offices and into a friendly environment for a positive learning experience. And even more important to you, seminars can deliver spectacular results for your business.

Television, radio, and print all tell your story. But sharing the experience of your story face to face will help your audience live it. If you can prepare a presentation that will arouse your audience's interest, you become a partner in the participants' growth. They grow. You grow. Everybody wins. The prospects for your business are endless.

By including prospecting seminars in your marketing mix, you are doing what good teachers have done for years. You are teaching, motivating, and moving people to action.

b. HOW THIS BOOK CAN HELP YOU

I recently received the following letter, which inspired me to write this book:

> Dear Barbara:
>
> A colleague of mine in Canada told me about the wonderful workshop you conducted for his organization on developing prospecting seminars. He was quite impressed with your presentation and is gungho about trying some seminars in the immediate future. I've tried them before and, quite frankly, I'm not convinced. They can be a logistical nightmare to organize, particularly for an organization that is already working to its maximum. They cut into valuable office time, and the success or failure of your efforts is subject to the whims of Mother Nature. So, what's all the hype about?
>
> Yours sincerely,
>
> W.S.

Seminars To Build Your Business is the result of many years of planning seminars for my company and clients. Thanks to that experience, I know what works and what doesn't. Furthermore, I have had the opportunity to watch others try to cope with the details that go into hosting a successful seminar. It looks easy from the outside, but once you get into the thick of it, the details can be overwhelming.

Consider this book your personal guide through the maze of activities needed to develop a successful prospecting seminar. It is a step-by-step approach which you can use to unravel its mysteries. As well, I provide a master checklist that you are welcome to photocopy and use when planning *your* seminar.

Each chapter covers a different step in the process. The chapters are presented in chronological order so that you can plan a successful seminar by simply following the order of the book:

In chapter 2 you will learn how to set your objectives. A seminar is a business activity, and as with any other business activity, you need to establish some firm guidelines on which to base your decisions.

Chapter 3 covers logistics. Here is where many planners become overwhelmed: too many details, not enough time.

Chapter 4 covers seminar marketing. There is no point holding a seminar if nobody shows up.

Chapter 5 deals with sponsorship. There is more than one way to soften the financial bite. Often you will have opportunities to work with other companies that can help you financially as well as promotionally.

Chapter 6 explains the use of guest speakers. If you choose to have someone else other than yourself speak at your seminar, this chapter is a must-read.

Chapter 7 is about making presentations. If you decide to deliver the talk yourself, but you have little experience, this is a crucial chapter. You will want to read this chapter even if you are using a guest speaker, as you will still need to act as master of ceremonies. You may even find that you have to present if that is part of your contingency plans.

Chapter 8 covers the skills you need to be a good networker. You have invited guests, so you want to make sure everyone is happy and that you make contact with as many people as possible.

Chapter 9 covers evaluation and follow-up. Once the seminar is over, your real work begins. In this chapter, you will learn how to evaluate your results to improve on future marketing and how to follow up to ensure you get the rewards you have worked for.

Chapter 10 is a few last words of wisdom that I hope will help you successfully conclude your journey to the promised land of prospecting seminars.

Appendix 1 provides success stories and examples of how companies have used prospecting seminars in unique ways. These include tips and tactics that will help give your seminar that special touch.

And finally, Appendix 2 is a recommended reading list to provide you with further resources.

2
SETTING YOUR SEMINAR OBJECTIVES

a. WHY SET OBJECTIVES?

According to Peter F. Drucker in his landmark book *Management: Tasks, Responsibilities, Practices,* "Objectives are the fundamental strategy of a business . . . . The basic definition of the business and of its purpose and mission . . . [has] to be translated into objectives. Otherwise, they remain insight, good intentions and brilliant epigrams which never become achievement."

Your prospecting seminar is a business. It involves profit (long-term), loss, risk, and potential, and just like all other facets of your business, it should be treated with great care. By setting realistic goals for your seminar, you increase your chances of success; ignoring this step can be a recipe for failure.

Here are some of the reasons to set objectives.

1. To provide a focus

Hosting a successful seminar involves looking after a tremendous amount of detail. At each stage, from initial planning to final execution, you will need to make choices, and each choice will move you in a certain direction. Sometimes the choice will be obvious, but at other times, there will be several choices and none of them — or all of them — may look good.

By having well-thought-out objectives, you will keep yourself focused and on the right path, making the right decisions.

2. To allocate resources

A prospecting seminar is just one of several marketing tools that will help you build your business. Allocating sufficient resources to achieve maximum benefit from the seminar will greatly enhance your chances of success. If you spread yourself too thin, chances are that you will come away from your seminar empty-handed.

Understanding your objectives will help you focus the appropriate amount of time, energy, and money on your seminar.

3. To schedule the right time

After setting realistic objectives and clearly defining your target audience (discussed later in this chapter, and in further detail in chapter 4), your timing decisions will become obvious. For example, if you are planning a retirement seminar and your target audience travels extensively in the winter, you would not hold a seminar in January. If you are recruiting for a university whose classes begin in September, don't wait for August to hold the seminar.

Having considered the season, you also need to look at the appropriate time of day. Should your seminar be in the morning, afternoon, or evening? Which day of the week is best? Are you more likely to get higher attendance at the beginning of the week or in the middle of the week? Should you schedule your seminar on the weekend?

Understanding your objectives and your target audience will make all these questions easier to answer.

4. To recognize opportunities

The key to a successful seminar is to focus on your primary objective. As you will learn later in this chapter, there are at least 15 possible objectives from which to choose.

Focusing on one does not mean you will not pay attention to the others, but by being aware of all possible objectives, you have the option of taking advantage of opportunities as they come up.

Understanding your objectives helps you identify hidden opportunities. With your primary objectives clearly articulated, you can see which opportunities will move you closer to your goal and which will lead you astray.

5. To stay motivated

Whatever your business, when you first began, you likely spent the bulk of your time marketing. In fact, it may have seemed like that was all you did. As your marketing activities started to pay off, you divided your time among other priorities such as customer service, production, finance, and administration.

To ensure that your business continues to thrive, you must be constantly on the lookout for new and exciting marketing opportunities. Running a seminar is a great marketing tool, but once you begin, you will realize that it takes a great deal of effort. You may at times wonder if it is all worth it. If you have set your objectives clearly, the answer will be obvious.

Objectives help keep you going when you'd rather kick off your shoes and curl up with a good book or watch television.

b. OBJECTIVE SETTING: A THREE-PART PROCESS

Setting objectives is a three-part process: defining what you want, identifying who you want it from, and establishing how you will achieve measurable results. Each part is an integral part of your seminar planning.

1. Defining what you want

Someone once said, "Unless you have defined what you want, you will never really know if you have got it."

Your first step in defining your objectives is to define clearly what you want from your seminar. You need to set one *primary objective* and two or three *secondary objectives*. Here are some of the most common reasons for conducting a seminar:

- *Obtain sales leads.* This is one of the most common seminar objectives. If you run your seminar professionally, you have an opportunity to set up appointments with prospects for future sales calls.

- *Sell materials and related products.* If your collateral materials have a short sales cycle, making back-of-the-room sales is a realistic objective. Once participants have met you and heard your information, they are usually more receptive to buying from you. (See Appendix 2 for more information.)

- *Advertise your Web site.* Your Web site can provide attendees with additional information which they can review at their leisure after the seminar.

- *Collect testimonials.* At the end of the seminar, ask for participant comments and permission to use these comments in future promotions. There is nothing like endorsements to boost your attendance figures.

- *Build your data base.* I always ask participants for names of friends and colleagues who may be interested in future seminars. If you have done your job well, gathering additional names is easy.

- *Attract media attention.* The media can be powerful allies if handled properly. A successful seminar can result in editorial coverage in local newspapers, magazines, television, and radio.

- *Showcase and demonstrate your expertise.* It's one thing to let people know through brochures and other collateral material what you do, but at a seminar you have the opportunity to show a group of targeted people that you really know your stuff.

- *Establish yourself as an industry spokesperson.* There are many benefits to increasing your visibility within an industry. Your seminar gives you a platform to begin your campaign to raise your profile within your industry.

- *Identify yourself as a consultant.* If people think your only business is selling products and services, here is your chance to change that perception. During your seminar, you can explain that your services also include consultation.

- *Gain name recognition.* When people think of your products or services, whose name springs to mind? You want people to associate your type of product or service with your name and call you before calling a competitor. A seminar can help you accomplish this. You build name recognition not only with the people who attend but also with those who received your promotional materials and could not attend. Having your name linked with a specific topic may spark an interest in people to call you for more information or to watch out for your next seminar.

- *Increase awareness of all your services.* Increasing public awareness is a longer-range objective. By hosting a seminar, you are letting a targeted group of people know about your business so that they can call on you if they need your services sometime in the future.

- *Promote your place of business.* Running a seminar in your own establishment will bring to your facility people who may have not considered coming before. Your place of business now becomes a destination. Bookstores do this all the time. Travel agents, clothing designers, and beauty salon operators have successfully used seminars to encourage prospective clients to visit their premises.

- *Support dealers and distributors.* A number of my clients have run seminars in partnership with their dealers or distributors. While my clients were not actively looking for leads or sales, the seminar helped to boost their distributors' business.

- *Recruit dealers and distributors.* Seeing you "live and in color" is a great way to encourage potential dealers or distributors to consider adding your products or services to their businesses. A seminar will give them the chance to see how you build rapport with clients.

- *Conduct market research.* What are good future seminar topics? Are you marketing to the right audience? What are the most effective marketing ideas? What do people think about your products and services? These are just some of the questions you can answer by including a bit of information gathering in your seminar plans.

2. Identifying your audience

Once you know what you want, you need to ask yourself who you want it from. In other words, you need to define your audience. This is the second step in defining your objectives.

You may think that your audience is simply "everyone" because of the broad appeal of your products or services. But even if your audience is drawn from a wide cross-section of the population, you must understand that this group does not consist of one homogeneous mass but rather of clearly definable groups of people.

Many entrepreneurs choose an audience they are most familiar with for their initial seminars. Former teachers might choose to sell to teachers, doctors to doctors, and so on. This approach makes a great deal of sense since you want to begin your business targeting a group with which you are comfortable. As you develop more seminars, you may want to approach other groups.

Another way to define your audience is by demographic and psychographic profiles. Population profiles can be found in government statistics, industrial surveys, and media sources.

Demography is the study of human populations. Demographic information is a statistical profile of particular population groups. The kind of demographic information you will want to collect will depend on your business, product, and goals. Traditional demographic information includes age, sex, income, buying patterns, family size, household income, education, and occupation. (See chapter 4 for more information on using demographics in your marketing.)

The term *psychographics* refers to the behavior patterns of consumers. It includes recreational activities, lifestyle choices, entertainment preferences, vacation choices, and family makeup, as well as personal opinions and attitudes on economic, social, and political topics. Psychographic information can help you zero in on your target group's specific needs with more precision than you would be able to if you relied only on straight demographics.

For example, when organizing a time-share seminar, participants' lifestyles are a major consideration. When planning an alternative medicine seminar, participants' attitudes toward traditional medicine are important.

If you can create a profile for each group of people you think will make up your audience, you can then answer the five Ws: Who, What, Where, When, and Why, which will help focus your planning and make your seminars more meaningful.

(a) **Who** will inspire the most confidence in your audience? Some people feel more comfortable with people their own age. They may look skeptically at people who appear too young to be knowledgeable, or they may label others as too old and out-of-date. In other cases, age is not a consideration at all.

13

The people you choose as assistants at your seminars should be those your audience will respect and feel comfortable with.

(b) **What** topic will generate the most interest? The topic and how you present it will depend on your target audience. If your specialty is travel, for example, you will want to develop a topic that will appeal to a certain segment of the population. A series of seminars might be best. Subjects may include singles' cruises, educational tours, hiking expeditions, and opportunities for extended vacations. It all depends on your audience.

(c) **Where** should you hold the seminar? The venue you choose must be convenient and accessible. If your audience lives in the country, an urban site may not be as attractive as a suburban or rural one. Your audience will also dictate the amenities that your venue will need to have, such as accessibility, acoustics, public transportation, and parking.

(d) **When** is the best time to hold a seminar? If your audience is part of the business community, an early morning breakfast meeting or early evening seminar may be best. For retirees, the middle of the day may be more attractive.

(e) **Why** will your targeted audience want to attend your seminar? This question goes to the heart of your planning. It is imperative that you understand your audience as best you can in order to provide programming that will encourage audience participation.

3. Quantifying your objectives

The final step in defining your objectives is to ensure that your objectives are measurable and that your targets are as realistic as possible. Your objectives should provide motivation, stimulation, and a realistic goal. According to Drucker, "your objectives can become the basis and the motivation for work and achievement."

Think about your objectives falling into one of two categories: sales or communication. Sales objectives are shorter term and deal with either direct sales or gathering leads. In contrast, communication objectives are usually longer term and include goals such as attracting media attention and gaining name recognition. In setting objectives, you may want to consider your sales objectives as primary and communication objectives as secondary.

Sales objectives are easier to measure. After the seminar, you can simply count the number of people who are either immediate buyers or who are leads for future business. If your goal is immediate business, you can arrange for your support staff to spend time with the participants after the seminar and sell your products or services on-site. However, if your objective is to generate leads, you will want to spend time working the floor.

A word of warning: If you try to accommodate both immediate and future sales by yourself, you risk not being successful with either. For example, if you want to gather leads, you should be spending a minimum amount of time with each participant. If someone wants to buy immediately and you have to stop networking to write up the order, you may lose other leads. If your goal is to gather leads, arrange for an associate to assist anyone who wants to make an immediate purchase, leaving you free to talk to as many people as possible.

Communication objectives are harder to measure. Building an image or establishing credibility, while important, is harder to quantify. Six months after attending your seminar, a journalist may approach you for a story, which then takes another three months to appear in print. It may be another month before you see any results from the article. Because communication objectives are longer term, you must choose two or three communication objectives as secondary objectives. These objectives do not directly affect your overall seminar planning, but it is important for you to track their eventual impact.

You can measure the effectiveness of your communication goals by having participants complete comment sheets before leaving the seminar or by conducting a postseminar telephone survey. Ask questions about the impact of your message, your business's image, and the participant's perception of your knowledge of the topic.

Setting realistic objectives for your seminars can be difficult. Particularly at the beginning, much of your goal setting will be guesswork. However, as you conduct more seminars, you will get better at guesstimating. Keeping accurate records of your seminars is important so that your decisions will grow to be based on experience rather than on guesswork.

And, finally, as with everything else in life, remember that there will always be external variables to consider, such as the weather, timing, and competing activities. In your planning, try to anticipate the impact these variables may have on a realistic assessment of your goals.

Once your goals are set, you are ready to tackle the seminar logistics.

3
THE LOGISTICS OF YOUR SEMINAR:
DETAILS, DETAILS, DETAILS

When your seminar is over and your guests look back on the event, what will they talk about? You hope it will be how effective the speaker was, how interesting the content of the presentation was, and how smoothly and professionally everything seemed to run. But if some of the details in the planning steps were neglected or poorly executed, you can be sure that this will be foremost in their minds. Lack of attention to detail can jeopardize the best seminars in the world. Good organization and preplanning are the keys to success.

Recently, I attended a seminar held by a nationally recognized speaker. It was in a hotel that had divided its ballroom in two. One side was for the seminar; the other was for a meeting of a very enthusiastic political group whose speaker was working the audience into a frenzy. It was literally a roaring success, while our seminar was a disaster as our speaker tried his best to speak over the noise.

In another seminar I attended, we were stuck in a room where the heat was on at full blast and nobody knew how to turn it down. In yet another, we were in a divided room with one set of light switches. When our neighbors dimmed the lights for their slide presentation, ours dimmed as well.

Under these types of conditions, it's impossible to pay attention to the speaker. And it all comes down to logistics. You have to accept that you can never anticipate every detail, but if you plan well, you can anticipate 95% of the potential problems and then have time to deal with anything unexpected.

In this chapter, I cover the many considerations of planning a seminar. I point out the common pitfalls and offer some time-saving and money-saving ideas.

Rather than trying to digest everything in one reading, you may want to review the Seminar Planning Master Checklist at the end of this chapter and concentrate on those areas that concern you the most. The checklist outlines all the steps of organizing a successful seminar, and you can use it to record all your seminar activities.

Whether you use this checklist or devise your own, always remember, don't leave anything to memory: *write everything down.* Logistical planning means coordinating a tremendous amount of information; missing any element could spell disaster.

If other people are helping you plan your seminar, it is also important to create — and use — a master list of roles and responsibilities. At one meeting I attended, two people were in charge of planning. One was an employee of the company that was putting on the seminar and the other was a volunteer recruited to help out. Each thought the other was taking care of the logistics, and consequently, the seminar developed into a nightmare: no microphone, no coffee service, and a speaker who arrived 20 minutes late. If the two planners had communicated and laid out each person's roles and responsibilities, these oversights would have been avoided. The lesson to learn from this is to use a planning sheet outlining the roles and responsibilities of each person on the team — and update it regularly. Sample #1 is a simple Roles and Responsibilities form you can adapt to your circumstances for this purpose.

Depending on the complexity of your seminar, you should start planning no later than eight weeks before the seminar. Some seminars require as much as four to six months to plan.

SAMPLE #1
SEMINAR PLANNING SHEET —
ROLES AND RESPONSIBILITIES

Task	Name	Action
Site selection		
Room reservation		
Audiovisual equipment		
Refreshments		
Marketing		
Invitations		
Guest-speaker selection		
Speaker coordination		
Registration		
Handout material		
Gifts		
Evaluations		
Disbursements		
Room monitor		
Follow-up letters		

a. SELECTING YOUR SEMINAR TOPIC

The primary reason people attend seminars is to learn something. Certainly, high-profile speakers will draw crowds by virtue of their names alone, but guests need content as well as name recognition. In other words, they want the steak *and* the sizzle.

Choosing the right topic is a crucial step in planning your seminar. It can in fact be viewed as more than a logistic. Your topic will become the focus of all your marketing. The right topic will appeal to your specific audience at the right time, which means that the topic must be as targeted as possible. If you try to cover too much material, or if your topic is too vague, you will dilute the impact of your seminar marketing, and of your seminar.

What is the right topic? The answer lies in a clear understanding of your audience. Answer this question: "How can my products or services be of most benefit to my targeted audience?"

If you start by listing the features and benefits of your products or services, you are on the wrong track. You are approaching it from your own point of view. Instead, you should be thinking about your products or services from the participants' points of view. Do they care if your services have all sorts of investment options or do they need to make their investment decisions quickly in order to qualify for the current taxation year? Do they want to talk about winter vacation properties in the middle of the winter when they have already made their vacation plans or would it be better talking to them in the summer or fall when they are still making their winter plans? Do they care about the benefits of becoming involved in a multilevel marketing concept when they are actively and happily engaged in a meaningful vocation? Do they want to buy franchises when they have just bought their first homes and are mortgaged to the eyeballs?

Think about what is important to your targeted audience and the effect of external factors on it. You have spent considerable time identifying your audience, but you have not spent as much time examining the effect of other factors on members of the audience. Some of these external factors include understanding local politics, labor issues, large-scale layoffs, development and environmental issues, announcements by local industry, or change in government policies. The topic you choose should help the members of your audience see a benefit, perhaps to make more money, keep the money they have, change their lifestyles, learn a new skill, or develop their potential for personal growth.

To know how all these factors will affect your audience, you must keep in touch with your community. By reading newspapers, joining local organizations, and talking to people, you will develop a good understanding of the mood of your audience, which will help you focus your topic to suit.

b. TIMING YOUR SEMINAR RIGHT

Regardless of general interest in your topic, some issues have greater appeal when they are linked with a timely event. A nonprofit organization wanting to raise funds for a Christmas blitz, planned a seminar in November when its audience could be motivated to take action. A water softener company took advantage of a major construction initiative that would greatly affect the quality of the local water system. Knowing in advance about the announcement, it planned a seminar within the month and attracted a huge audience. As a result, many residents signed contracts with the company. Multilevel marketing companies offering career options successfully ran seminars in locations after a major industry announced it was downsizing.

Tax planning seminars tend to run throughout the year, but the greatest interest occurs between November and January, when filing deadlines are quickly approaching.

Many of these seminars would not have been as success-ful if they had run at another time. And good timing isn't linked just to your topic: there are other external factors to consider. For example, your potential participants may not want to miss a major sporting event or a political rally. As well, you must consider cultural factors. There's no point trying to attract a Jewish audience on Yom Kippur or a Christian audience on Christmas Day. This may seem obvi-ous, but more than one seminar has been ruined because the planner neglected to look at his or her calendar.

Here are ten tips that have helped seminar planners avoid costly timing mistakes:

- Avoid holidays, as well as the day before and after a holiday. Whether the holiday be national, regional, local, or religious, people will want to spend the day before and/or the day after either with their families or in the office.

- Be aware of political events such as elections or spe-cial local events such as fairs.

- Research has shown that the best months to run a seminar are April, May, September, and October. However, seminars directly related to events at spe-cific times of the year may do well in months other than these.

- Try to schedule your seminar on Tuesday, Wednes-day, or Thursday to avoid the weekend, unless your topic draws an audience that is readily available on weekends.

- Consider weather conditions that could affect atten-dance. If you live in a cold climate, avoid holding your seminar in December, January, or February, when you run the risk of having to cancel it because of a major storm. If you live in a hot climate, avoid holding your seminar in July or August, when the weather may be unbearable.

- Be aware of other activities such as a jackpot lottery, when everyone stays home to see if he or she is holding the lucky number, or a major sporting event such as the World Series or the Super Bowl, when your audience will probably be glued to their television sets.

- Evening seminars are popular because they give business clients an opportunity to spend the full day at work before attending. Early morning breakfast seminars or late afternoon meetings can also be productive for a business audience.

- If your target audience is seniors, a lunch-and-learn seminar can be very popular.

- Depending on the time of day that you schedule the seminar, select the location convenient to the participants' residences or work.

c. SELECTING THE RIGHT SITE

Choosing the right site for your seminar is important to its success; the decision of which facility to use should not be taken lightly. Don't jump at the first available facility. The choice of venues can be overwhelming, and there are many factors to consider. The first step is to do a site inspection. Think of the three As: Accessibility, Adaptability, and Affordability.

1. Accessibility

Is the site you are considering accessible to your target audience? In chapter 4 you will define the characteristics of your target audience both demographically and psychographically. Take this information and apply it to determining the right location. Some places will work well, some can be adjusted and made to work, and some are simply not suitable.

To begin, ask yourself these questions about your audience:

(a) Where do members of my target audience live and work?

(b) How do they commute?

(c) What kind of extracurricular activities are they involved in?

(d) What is their family makeup?

(e) What location would be most convenient for them?

These questions will reveal certain things about your target audience you might otherwise not have realized.

A client of mine was offered the use of a room in his local church to hold a seminar. It was a very pleasant facility and convenient to the area in which most of his target group lived. It was also free, which helped his budget a lot. However, his target market included people of the Jewish and Moslem faiths who were not comfortable spending time in a Christian church. He lost many prospective guests as a result.

Another client ran a seminar at the crossroads of two major traffic arteries leading from downtown into a residential neighborhood where a large part of his target audience lived. He thought the location would attract people on their way home from work. What he overlooked was that a large part of his audience was made up of single parents who had to stop to pick up their children on the way home, which made his chosen location inconvenient.

Considering accessibility also means anticipating any special needs that your audience may have. For example, if your guests use wheelchairs or walkers, ensure your meeting room has wheelchair access and a handicapped washroom nearby. Inform the people staffing the registration desk of any special needs so each person requiring extra attention can be taken care of when he or she arrives.

If accessibility is an issue, try to reserve a room on the main floor and avoid a room at the end of a long corridor. Also, ensure that public transportation to the facility is available and that the hours of operation are noted in your seminar program.

Understanding your audience and their lifestyle needs will lead you to the most suitable site.

2. Adaptability

Is the site you are considering adaptable to the seminar and the specific needs of your audience? Your site should have all the amenities you are looking for. A free place can turn out to be very expensive if it isn't equipped to handle the type of people you are attracting. You could get stuck with a lot of extra costs or, even worse, a small turnout.

The best way to ensure that your prospective site can accommodate the needs of your seminar guests is to inspect it personally. When you do so, use a checklist of the amenities that are important to your target audience. Ensure there is elevator access, on-site parking, handicapped access, washrooms, coat check, telephones, security, catering facilities, and restaurant availability.

Walk around the facility and note the appearance of the reception area, the grounds, and the meeting rooms. Are they neat and clean?

If the building is under renovation, as is commonplace in any public facility, request that no work be done during your seminar. You don't want to be disturbed by the unexpected sound of jackhammers in the next room. Ensure that this request is written into your confirmation letter (discussed later in this chapter).

Check the schedule of events already booked for the day on which you plan to hold your seminar to ensure there are no activities that may compete for the time or attention of your audience. A charity bingo, for example, may draw your audience away from your seminar. Having managed to get people to your seminar site, you don't want some other event sidetracking them.

Ask the facility manager if the rooms adjacent to your prospective room have been rented and if so, what functions are taking place in them. This will provide a clue to the noise competition you may encounter.

Look around the room itself. Is it inviting? Is the lighting good? How are the acoustics? Check the ceiling height. Some people find rooms with low ceilings claustrophobic.

If there is an exercise facility on the premises, make sure the room you plan to use is not nearby. The smell of chlorine from a pool, or the sound of people working out, can be a distraction at the least!

Check the proximity of the kitchen to your room. Can you hear the kitchen activity or smell tonight's dinner?

Is a business service center available for your use? If you run into last-minute emergencies, you will want to be near telephones, photocopiers, and fax machines.

If your time is limited or your budget doesn't allow for an on-site inspection, be sure to have a detailed telephone conversation with the facility manager to ensure he or she is clear about your requirements and goals for the seminar. Ask for the correct name and spelling of the facility and the room you have booked so you can include them on your seminar invitations and marketing material. Ask the facility manager to send you a map along with your room confirmation.

Finally, *make sure you get everything in writing.* Sample #2 is an example of a letter of confirmation for booking a meeting room.

INTERNATIONAL TRAINING AND MANAGEMENT
16436 Shaw's Creek Road
Terra Cotta, ON L0P 1N0

To: Joan Chan,   *Date:* August 30, 199-
Catering Manager
Conference Centre,
1600 Northwest Boulevard,
Seattle, WA 78910

Meeting date: November 25, 199-
Meeting hours: 7:00 p.m. – 10 p.m.
Room set up and ready for use at: 6:00 p.m.
Name of room: Ballroom A
Post meeting as: Ten Tips for Women Travelers

Food and beverage service:

Time	Refreshments	Quantity
6:45 p.m.	coffee, tea, cookie tray	50
Water station:	50 glasses	8 pitchers of water

Refresh room at: 8:30 p.m.

Please provide the following audiovisual equipment:

1 Microphone
1 Overhead projector
0 Slide projector
1 Flip chart
0 35mm projector

1 Screen
0 VCR
2 Display tables
1 Registration table
1 Coat rack
– Other _____

The following are the agreed-on charges:

Room rental: $250 + taxes
Food and beverage: $4 per person + taxes
Audiovisual: $85 + taxes
Gratuities: 15%
Other:

Terms of payment: **Payable on receipt of invoice**

Special instructions: Set room up for 50 people
in banquet style, six per table, and two extra
chairs at side.

Please sign below and return one copy for our files.

Acknowledged by _____

Date _____

3. Affordability

The final criterion is whether the site is affordable. And remember, affordable doesn't necessarily mean the cheapest. You generally get what you pay for.

You want the facility to be compatible with the image you are trying to achieve. Some places look shabby while others may appear ostentatious. There are many different facilities to choose from besides traditional hotel banquet or meeting rooms. For example, many universities and community colleges are opening up their classrooms for conferences. These are typically inexpensive rooms, but they may not be adequately supplied. One facility I used could not provide markers for the flip chart.

Corporations often rent out their corporate training centers to outside groups. Such centers tend to be lower in price than hotels. In addition, the rooms that are specifically designed for conferences and meetings tend to be better equipped. Such a facility also offers a more serious learning environment: you won't find a product launch, charity bingo, or wedding shower in the next room!

Check your neighborhood for other facilities such as public schools, libraries, and churches or synagogues (if appropriate) for meeting space. Often retail outlets such as bookstores have meeting spaces available for programs and welcome the opportunity to bring people into their businesses. Or one of your suppliers might offer you seminar space in its showroom at no charge. Always do a site inspection of such venues. Look at the lighting, temperature, seating space, washrooms, and other amenities. One of my clients ended up with a room that had indirect lighting to highlight the supplier's products but was completely inadequate for a seminar. At the last minute, spot lights were brought into the room which only made it worse for the audience who now had to deal with glaring pools of light reflecting off all the walls.

Whatever facility you choose, remember that you are responsible for coordinating your meeting. Don't assume that just because a facility rents out meeting space and advertises its proficiency in running meetings that you can leave the details to its staff. The ultimate success of your function rests with you and the amount of advanced planning you have done with the meeting coordinator. You must have a healthy respect for Murphy's Law: anything that can go wrong will go wrong. While it may seem unfair, if one thing goes wrong in an otherwise smoothly run seminar, your participants will invariably remember this one detail long after the seminar is over.

d. NEGOTIATING ON THE FACILITY

Your power to negotiate is all a matter of timing. If you talk to a facility manager when every other space in town is rented, there will be very little to negotiate. But if you talk to that same manager when there is a glut of available space, you will likely be able to negotiate favorable terms. The cost of the room is sometimes negotiable, as are audiovisual equipment rentals, the catering, and use of hotel amenities.

Make sure you know what will be included in your costs. Look for any hidden costs, such as an extra payment for coat checking. Some hotels have a policy of linking function-room rentals to their regular guest rooms. For example, a hotel might prefer renting seminar space to you if you can also guarantee that some of your guests will be staying overnight at that hotel.

The trick to negotiating is to not be afraid to ask — for anything. If you are up-front from the beginning and set out the parameters of your budget, the facility manager can often come up with creative solutions that work well for both of you.

Be sure to confirm every detail in writing, including the following:

- What is included in the cost of the room

- What amenities are supplied free of charge (e.g., pens, paper, water)

- What additional charges apply, such as gratuities and taxes

- What the last date to guarantee the number of participants for catering is

- The time the room will be ready

- The time you need to be out of the room

- Who will do room setup and how it will be set up

- Catering requirements

- Audiovisual requirements

- Credit application, if necessary

- Storage available if you need to deliver supplies ahead of time

It is also important to think about liability issues when you sign an agreement. I remember a famous lawyer telling me that *everything* we do in life has legal consequences. Most of the time, these consequences are not serious, but you need to be aware of the potential issues of legal liability when running seminars.

"Your agreement is a legal contract and should be taken seriously," warns Tony Pillard, president of the Hotel Association of Canada. "The meeting industry is doing well and facility space is tight. Contracts must be adhered to. Before you sign, read the contact carefully and make sure you understand what you are committing to. There are specific cancellation clauses with deadlines clearly spelled out. If you guarantee 50 people for coffee and only 20 show up, expect to be charged for the full 50."

While the facility, not you, is liable for accidents that happen on its premises, that doesn't mean that you will remain untouched. We live in a litigious society, and if an accident occurs, chances are that you will be part of any legal action.

Liability insurance is fairly inexpensive and can often be bought as a rider to your existing business insurance policy. If you plan to run a number of seminars, talk to your insurance agent and discuss the possibility of adding liability coverage.

e. SETTING UP THE ROOM

Uppermost in your mind when planning your seminar should be the comfort of your guests. Uncomfortable guests result in an unresponsive audience. The room and environment are crucial for your success.

1. Room comfort

First, think about the size of the room you need. You need to do more than just determine how many guests you can squeeze in. Will you be using a raised stage or podium? How much space do you need for audiovisual equipment?

Next, think about how the chairs can be placed. Are pillars or other obstacles preventing people from having a clear view?

Is the lighting adequate for the size of the room? Are there windows, allowing for natural light? Reflective surfaces such as mirrors can cause eye fatigue and reduce concentration. If the room has mirrors, set the chairs so that your audience is not facing them.

Climate control is also an important consideration. Often, seminars rooms are either too hot or too cold. The temperature will have an effect on your audience's ability to concentrate. If the heating and air conditioning controls are under lock and key and accessible only to the facility's engineer, make sure you have his or her pager number.

Send a seating plan to the caterer and confirm the number of seats you require. Most hotels and convention centers have a good supply of furniture for any seminar setup. If you chose a legion hall, sports center, or other facility with staff less experienced in running seminars, you may have to look to a private furniture rental company for seating. These companies have a wide variety of furniture available and usually offer delivery and pickup service. You can rent almost everything you need, including cups, saucers, coffee urns, and coat racks.

2. Registration area

Position your registration table just inside the room, close to the main entrance, or else just outside the room. You want your registration table to be obvious to your guests but positioned so that latecomers will not disturb your speaker and guests.

The registration table should have a sign with the name of the seminar and the registration details. If you are using name badges, they can be placed in alphabetical order on the table. If your guests are filling in their own name badges, make sure you have felt markers available and enough room for guests to write. Those who have preregistered can be handled fairly quickly by simply checking off their names on a master list.

Last-minute registrations will take more time but can be streamlined if you have registration forms available at the desk to capture all the information of latecomers. If there are more than two guests at this desk, you may encounter some congestion, so consider having two tables, one for preregistered guests and another for walk-in registrations. There should be enough room around the registration table to allow for an easy flow of traffic.

3. Room setup

There are five typical seating arrangements used for public meetings and seminars:

(a) *Theater style* works well with large groups (see Figure #1). Your audience is seated in rows, which is ideal if you plan limited audience interaction and minimal note-taking.

(b) *Banquet style* seats people at round tables. This is a good setup if you plan to have a lot of small group discussions (see Figure #2). Semicircular seating is even better so that no one's back is to the presenter.

(c) *Classroom style* seats participants behind a table, giving them room to take notes but providing minimal room for small group interaction. It is a good setup for groups of 30 to 60 people, where there will be a lot of note-taking (see Figure #3). The standard for comfortable classroom seating is two people per six-foot table, although hotels often seat three people at a six-foot table.

(d) *Chevron or herringbone style* is similar to the classroom style setup, with the tables in a repeated V formation (see Figure #4).

(e) *Hollow square or U-shape* setups work well with smaller groups. Both styles put people in face-to-face contact, which encourages them to interact with each other and promotes better discussions. It also gives them ample room for note-taking (see Figures #5 and #6).

Here are a few additional tips for setting up the room:

• Set out chairs for the number of guests you are expecting — no more. You should plan for a certain number of "no-shows" and for some that will arrive at the last minute. It is better to have additional chairs available in an adjacent room and to quickly set them

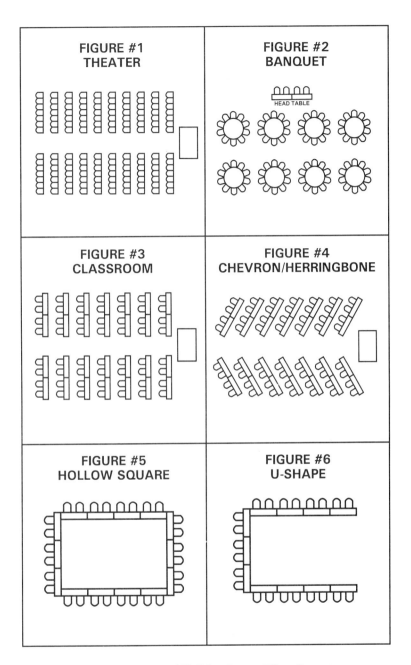

Reproduced by permission of Holiday Inn on King, Toronto

up after extra guests arrive than to have a room with empty chairs.

People tend to sit scattered in a room set up with too many chairs, draining energy from the room and affecting the dynamics. When people sit close together, they interact more, laugh more, are more receptive, take a more active role, and enjoy the seminar more.

- Encourage participants to sit near the front. People tend to avoid sitting in the front row, but your registration staff can encourage people to sit at the front by "selling" some of the benefits of doing so (e.g., the room will likely be full, so sitting at the front will allow them to see better and hear every word the presenter says).

- Have the facility pipe music into the room through an in-house system (if possible) or play music on your own portable system. Having your guests enter a room filled with pleasant sounds creates a positive atmosphere.

- If your seminar has a theme, consider decorating the room to reinforce it. Travel posters, charts and graphs, streamers, and balloons all add to the impact of the seminar. On the other hand, if you overdo the decorations, you will detract from the mood of your seminar. (Also be sure to check with the facility manager that you can decorate as you choose.)

- Set up a refreshment table at the back or side of the room. If possible, avoid setting it against a wall, which will prevent guests from mingling around the table. If the table is open on all sides, there will be less chance of guests having to line up to get a cup of coffee.

It is also important to specify with the catering manager the exact times for refreshment breaks so that your seminar will not be interrupted with the sound of clinking coffee cups.

- Position an information table with additional hand-out material at the side of the room. Decide whether you want to put out your material before the seminar or hold it back until the end. Handing it out after the seminar eliminates the tendency of some people to read during the presentation. On the other hand, having it available before the seminar gives your guests something to do while they are waiting for you to begin.

- Arrange for a small table at the front of the room to hold your speaker's notes or overhead transparencies.

- Inform the facility staff that you do not want telephone calls during the workshop, and instruct that any important messages be hand delivered. Unless instructed otherwise, the facility staff will put any telephone calls for you through to the room telephone. These often come at the most inopportune time and are very disruptive to your seminar.

  Also make sure the facility puts a restriction on the use of in-room telephones for long-distance calls or you may face large and unexpected expenses.

- And, finally, remembering Murphy, make sure you have a contact name in each relevant department in the facility, in case something goes wrong. Alternatively, have the name of a general contact who can help direct your request.

f. SIGNAGE

Think about what our world would be like without signs. There are signs that tell you where to go, which way to get there, and what to do once you are there. We use signs to help direct us through our day, and signage is just as important for your seminar.

Start by driving up to the facility where your seminar will be held, pretending that you have never been there before. Ask yourself what signs helped you find the facility with the greatest ease. Keep these in mind as you give your guests directions to the seminar.

Sometimes, hotels and convention facilities will permit promotion on a lighted marquee, electronic directory, or signboard outside the building. The wording you use on these signs should be what your audience will recognize. Guests may not easily recognize your business's name but may be familiar with the seminar topic or the name of the guest speaker you have advertised — so that's what should be on the sign. For example, a sign saying "Nutritional Information Seminar" may be more effective than one saying "Jane Doe's Seminar."

If the facility has a daily meeting directory in the front lobby, your sign there should also refer to the seminar topic or guest speaker.

A sign with an arrow pointing to the seminar room should be placed as close as possible to the front door. Every time you have to change a direction, a sign should be pointing your guests in the right direction. (Signs can be made of white board and mounted on an easel.)

If the facility has an elevator, a sign should be placed just outside the elevator in the lobby, indicating the floor and room in which the seminar is being held. Another sign should be placed outside the elevator on the floor on which the seminar is taking place.

Finally, right at the seminar room, you should have one sign indicating the registration area and perhaps a larger sign or banner proclaiming the name of the seminar. Ask your sponsors to provide large signs or banners to be placed inside the room. (More information on finding sponsors is provided in chapter 5.)

As you tour the facility, make notes of all the places for which you will need signs so that you are prepared with the proper signage the day of the seminar.

g. FOOD AND BEVERAGE

You will need to offer your seminar participants some type of refreshment. This can be as simple as a cup of coffee or something as substantial as sandwiches or a complete meal. Choosing what to serve will depend on the time of the seminar, its length, and the image you want to present.

Coffee (regular and decaffeinated), tea, juice, and soft drinks are expected any time of day. You may want to include muffins or croissants for morning seminars, light sandwiches at noon, fruit or cookies mid-afternoon, and cheese or other nibbles in the early evening.

In a two-and-a-half hour seminar, there will probably be one break (around half time). Refreshments should be available before the seminar begins and during the break. If a morning seminar goes beyond two-and-a-half hours to a full morning, you may want to consider a continental breakfast or light lunch. The rule is that if your seminar crosses a regular meal time, you should provide the meal. If your guests are coming late in the afternoon and you expect to keep them over the dinner hour, a light meal is appropriate.

You want your guests to leave with the impression that you care about them. Your choice of catering can reflect this. Be wary of serving alcohol, which sends a message that you are entertaining, not educating. Alcohol is not necessary at a seminar.

You do not want to create an image that says "I'm cheap," but you can still be economical in your food and beverage selections. For example, if you offer coffee and cookies, you can upgrade by serving gourmet or speciality coffees and handmade cookies.

Sometimes a little research will give you clues to the right catering. Talk to the catering manager if you are using a hotel or convention facility. Ask to see a sample of the caterer's work and photos of how the catering will be presented.

Finally, don't forget about possible dietary restrictions. Make sure you are prepared for some of the dietary requirements your audience may have. Be sure to have both decaffeinated coffee and herbal teas available for those who avoid caffeine. Be sensitive to certain food allergies as well. Peanuts are a common allergen, so avoid serving them. If you are serving a meal, offer vegetarian options.

h. PREREGISTRATION

The contract for the meeting facility is signed, the invitations out. Now you sit and wait to see who will show up. Wrong!

You need to know who will be attending well before the seminar date so that you can organize for your specific audience and make any needed changes to your plans. You do this by having your guests preregister.

On your invitations or in your advertisements, encourage people to preregister. Make it as easy as possible for people to reach you either through the mail or by providing a toll-free telephone and fax number or an e-mail address. Use the opportunity of preregistration to talk to each registrant. Keep a prepared registration sheet by the telephone and be ready to solicit the following information when the caller confirms his or her attendance:

- Name, occupation, age group
- Level of knowledge on the topic
- Reason for attending

- What specifically he or she is interested in hearing

- How he or she heard about the seminar (for future marketing)

- If he or she has any friends or acquaintances who might also appreciate receiving an invitation to the seminar

- If he or she has any special needs (e.g., dietary, building access)

- If he or she has any questions

If an assistant is answering the telephone for you, make sure the assistant knows all the details of the seminar and is able to answer any question that arises.

Anyone taking registration over the telephone — whether you or an assistant — should have a positive attitude. For many of your guests, this is their first contact with you, and you want to make sure the impression is a good one.

With the preregistration information in hand, you will be able to tailor your seminar to your audience. You can also confirm that you have booked the appropriate size of room, and that the catering and other amenities are satisfactory.

Confirm all registrations in writing. Provide each participant with the time, place, directions, and any other helpful, relevant information. This step will help create a positive impression with your guest before the seminar even begins.

Your confirmation can be on a predesigned form that is faxed, e-mailed, or mailed. Sample #3 is an example of a confirmation letter to guests.

i. PRESENTATION TOOLS

A host of tools are available that can boost the professional look of your presentation. Compare the impact of a person standing alone on a stage delivering a talk without the help of a microphone, overhead projector, VCR, computer, or flip

Ms. Lynda James
5000 Main Street
Seattle, WA 54321

Dear Ms. James,

We are pleased to confirm that you are registered for our seminar on Ten Tips For Women Travelers on Tuesday, November 25, 199-, at the Conference Centre, 1600 Northwest Boulevard, Seattle.

Registration starts at 6:45 p.m. outside Ballroom A on the ground floor. The seminar will start at 7:00 p.m. Come early to enjoy a cup of coffee and meet some of the other guests who will be attending.

We look forward to seeing you there. If you have any questions, please do not hesitate to call us at 1-800-555-4567.

Yours sincerely,

Barbara Siskind
Seminar Director

chart with that of a speaker who has carefully chosen some of these tools to add impact to the presentation. Who would you rather listen to?

Professional speakers know how important these tools are and carefully plan to use the right tools for their audience. You can visit an audiovisual equipment supplier to see demonstrations of the various options and determine which you feel most comfortable with.

Here is a quick guide to using the right presentation tool at the right time.

1. Microphones

Microphones are essential for groups larger than 40 people or for smaller groups if you have a soft voice. Stationary microphones work well if you are making a presentation from a podium. If you plan to move around the room during your presentation, consider using the handheld style of microphone with a long cord. If you don't want to worry about tripping over the cord, you might consider a wireless clip-on microphone (called a lavaliere microphone), which gives you complete freedom to move around and doesn't inhibit hand gestures. However, be forewarned that wireless microphones are more expensive, and you need to invest in a good quality one or you could be plagued with static and interference. And a word of caution: be sure to turn off the microphone during the breaks; you don't want everyone to hear what you are doing in the washroom while you freshen up!

Be sure to do a sound check before the seminar — while the technician is still in the room. Take the microphone and walk around to locate dead spots or areas where there is mechanical feedback. Make sure the sound level is high enough that you will be audible to those people sitting at the back of the room.

2. Flip charts

Flip charts are inexpensive and reliable; they don't involve any mechanics that can break down. Flip charts are a great tool to use if you want to write notes or draw diagrams for the group as you proceed through the seminar. As well, you can prepare flip chart pages ahead of time and simply turn to the appropriate page when needed.

However, a flip chart has limited use in large groups. If the audience can't read your writing, it can undermine your credibility. As well, inexpensive newsprint can tear easily and ink can bleed through onto the next sheet if you press too hard when you write.

If you do use a flip chart, use markers in primary colors for the best effect.

3. Overhead projectors

Overhead projectors can project an image onto a large screen with a minimum amount of hassle. There is very little that can go wrong with a projector except a light bulb burning out, and that is easily fixed, as most projectors have a second bulb in the carrying case. Make sure you check for the spare bulb when setting up the equipment and know how to change it quickly.

You can create dynamic overheads on transparencies using readily available presentation software programs. Your lettering for overheads should be in 18 to 24 point text in a readable font such as Helvetica or Times Roman. Avoid script and other fancy fonts such as Old English, which can be difficult to read.

It is also easy to incorporate cartoons, charts, and graphs into your presentations by using transparencies. Blank transparencies can be used to develop spontaneous charts or to emphasize important words.

Some speakers place their transparencies into cardboard frames, which can be purchased at an office supply store. The frames prevent the transparencies from sticking together and makes your presentation run more smoothly. It also provides a place to crib notes.

If you choose to use transparencies, keep in mind that they are there to help the audience follow along. Do not simply read what you have written on the transparencies: that is boring and a waste of time.

When you use an overhead, you do not need to dim the lights in order for people in the back row to be able to see the transparencies. Also, remember to turn off the overhead projector when you are between using transparencies so they don't become a distraction.

4. Slide projectors

Slides are a great way to create a visual sequence of events or tell a story. A projector is fairly simple to operate, and you can create sharp images easily. Slides create a greater impact than do transparencies and are a good tool to use for a formal presentation or if you have a very large audience. As well, a slide show can be easily adapted to various audiences by adding new slides or changing their order.

There are, however, some disadvantages to using slides. The lights need to be dimmed in order for the audience to see them clearly, which makes note-taking difficult. You also lose visual contact with your audience. And unless the slide show is compelling, your audience can become passive and drowsy.

Technical problems arise quite often with slide projectors. The light bulb can blow or the slide tray can jam, and it seems to be a law of nature that there is always one slide in backward or upside down.

All this means that it is important to rehearse your slide presentation. And if you do run into trouble, be ready to improvise. Don't stop the show and expect your audience to wait while you take 15 minutes to fix the problem.

5. VCRs

Videos are not meant to replace a live presenter, but they can provide a high-impact presentation in which you can combine sound, sight, and motion. You don't have to go to the expense and trouble of making your own video: professional videos are available for rental on a number of business topics. These use professional actors and can be highly entertaining. Imagine having John Cleese or the Muppets at your next seminar!

If you use a video presentation, make sure the tape is rewound and cued to the exact point you want it to begin. Adjust the volume and test it before the seminar. Make sure the clock is not flashing, as this will distract your audience from your presentation. You may need two monitors if you have a large group so that everyone can see clearly.

6. Multimedia

With the proper application of one of the many presentation software programs, you can develop a high-impact presentation that will create a leading-edge image for you and your business. Computer-assisted presentations offer the flexibility of manipulating statistical graphs and charts into easy-to-understand information. Many programs can be used with enhanced multimedia such as video and audio to add additional impact to your presentation.

When shopping for presentation software programs, be careful of those designed for someone who is more technically advanced than you. Some programs can be complicated to work and offer nothing more than frustration. One option is to hire a service company that can help you create your dynamic presentation, relieving you of the need to learn a new program.

Like anything else, these programs are just tools to enhance your presentation: they can't "do" your presentation for you. Make sure they are not too gimmicky, drawing attention away from your message. And when you are working on your budget, keep in mind that multimedia presentations involve the additional cost of purchasing or renting the equipment, which is more expensive than some of the other presentation tools discussed.

Many seminar facilities have their own audiovisual equipment while others rent from outside suppliers. When arranging for your equipment, check whether the technician will be on-site or on call. Batteries in microphones have been known to die in the middle of presentations, and light bulbs on projectors can blow and plunge your room into darkness. If the technician is not on-site, be sure to have a pager number so you can call for help if needed.

j. HANDOUT MATERIALS

Your seminar guests will expect to take something away with them to reinforce the material covered in the seminar and to help them develop a strategy for action. Well-prepared handout material serves this purpose and gives you another vehicle with which to promote your business.

Handouts are generally simple and inexpensive to reproduce, they leave your guests with a positive reminder of your presentation, and they are a handy reference for your guests after the seminar. Remember that your handout material may be passed around to other people, so make sure your name and telephone number are on the bottom of every page, along with a copyright notice which says that the work is copyrighted in your name (if it is). If you are using material other than your own, be sure to get permission to do so from the appropriate person.

Handouts are not useful if they are not prepared with thought and care. Avoid an overly busy look with too many different type styles or fonts. Check and double-check the text for spelling and grammatical errors. Ask someone to proofread everything for you: it is difficult to spot mistakes on material you've created yourself.

One proven method for developing handout material is to arrange it in the form of workshop notes, that is, information that can be completed by the guests as they follow along with the speaker. This technique improves your guests' attention span because they are doing more than just sitting and listening: they have an activity to complete. If you choose this approach, ensure that each participant has a pen to write with.

When arranging the pages, make sure they follow the same sequence as your presentation. Nothing is more distracting than seeing your audience flip through pages to find the reference for the point you are making. Develop your handout material so it is more than just a copy of the transparencies: include information that will be a useful reference *after* the seminar.

Include an evaluation form as part of the handout material. In chapter 9, I discuss various methods of evaluating your seminar. No matter which format you choose, make sure each of your guests complete an evaluation form before leaving.

Handout material can be sent out with the preregistration confirmation, given out when guests arrive, or offered as a take-away at the end of the seminar. If you send it out in advance, you can include a reminder to your guests to review it before they attend, which will help equalize the experience level of the audience. Often the sophistication of your audience may vary, which provides an extra challenge to you, the presenter. By giving everyone information in advance, you can assume some basic level of knowledge.

One drawback to giving out material ahead of time is that some people will assume they now have all the material you will be covering and so there is no value in attending. Be sure to mention that the handout is just a brief overview of what you will be covering at the seminar. You want to whet the participants' appetites to learn more. Also have extra copies at the seminar; inevitably, one or two guests will forget to bring theirs.

If you choose to distribute your material as the guests arrive, it can be included in your larger seminar package. The material helps participants focus on the seminar topic. While they are waiting for the rest of the guests to arrive, they can sit and read. The danger with this is that they will be reading and not networking with other participants. Also, if they don't complete the reading by the time the seminar starts, guests might ignore the speaker as they finish reading the material.

If you decide that you want to distribute your material after the seminar, your package will be a bit different. Rather than concentrating on the subject matter you covered during the seminar, you will want to focus more on an overview of both your seminar and your business. (No matter when you hand out seminar materials, you will want to develop this kind of general package as well.) As your guests leave, they can pick up their package containing collateral materials consisting of background information on the topic, handout material, an overview of your presentation, articles related to the topic, gifts donated by sponsors, and your brochure and business card.

Always keep in mind that your materials should be developed with the goal of leaving your guests with a positive feeling about you and the seminar they have attended.

k. DOOR PRIZES

Door prizes can provide a bit of fun to your seminar as well as boost attendance and keep your audience in their seats until the presentation is over. You should be careful when choosing a door prize to ensure that it attracts the right audience. Recently I went to a seminar sponsored by a travel company promoting a trip to Antarctica. The newspaper ad mentioned door prizes without indicating what they might be. There was a draw for T-shirts with penguins on the front. As luck would have it, I won a prize. Now every time I wear that shirt I am reminded of the seminar.

About 50 people attended this seminar. If the operator wanted to increase attendance, he could have offered a larger prize, such as a free trip to Antarctica, which would have boosted attendance but it is doubtful whether the quality of the audience would have been improved in proportion to the size.

Sponsors will often provide a prize in return for their name being attached to it. Some door prizes to consider include gift packages from local retailers, dinner at a well-known restaurant, theater passes, weekend trips, a barbecue, exercise equipment, books (particularly if your guest speaker is a published author), and limousine rides. Just about anything that your audience perceives as valuable or useful can serve as a door prize.

I. BUDGETING

A typical business budget consists of two broad categories: revenue and expenses. When you are budgeting for a prospecting seminar, you will be dealing with only one of these: your expenses. As discussed in chapter 1, a prospecting seminar must be considered as a cost of doing business — part of your marketing and development costs. Your real income happens once the seminar is over and you have an opportunity to convert new leads to business.

Prospecting seminars are only one marketing piece in your overall business plan. While each cost incurred needs to be justified as a good business decision, you can share some of these costs by partnering or soliciting the support of sponsors. I discuss sponsorships in detail in chapter 5.

Before planning your seminar, you want to determine what proportion of your overall marketing budget you will allocate to this activity. If this is your first seminar and you have no track record, this is hard to estimate. It's important to walk before you run, go slowly, and keep your plans modest. There is nothing wrong with organizing a seminar for which your costs are in the hundreds of dollars rather than the thousands. Once your feet are wet, you will be more confident in the outcome and be more willing to make the outlay that can yield higher results. Think of your first seminar as your test seminar.

Although you are spending hard dollars, remember that the rewards are not in direct cash but in leads and future business that will be generated from your prospecting seminar. Make sure you can cover the expenditures so as not to jeopardize your current bottom line while developing new business.

There are many hidden costs involved in running a seminar, and you want to develop a realistic budget to ensure there are no surprises later. While your office overhead for the seminar will be a percentage of your total office expenses, all other costs will depend on the scope of your seminar.

The following are questions to consider as you develop your budget:

- How many guests are you trying to attract?

- How are you planning to promote your seminar? Are you planning to send out printed invitations, produce a four-color brochure, or use a fax broadcast from your own computer?

- What is the best place to hold your seminar?

- What kind of refreshments are most suitable for the participants?

- What are your audiovisual requirements?

- How much material do you want participants to walk away with?

- Who will be making the presentation, you or a guest speaker?

- How will you handle all the seminar logistics?

Sample #4 is a basic outline you can use to prepare and track your expenditures. When the seminar is over, do a final accounting. Review the expenditures against new business generated.

Much of your new business will not happen immediately. Keep an ongoing record of the number of new leads for 3, 6, and 12 months to determine the effectiveness of your seminar. Track your results in terms of the number of new leads, and compare this to the new business actually attained. By doing this, you will also be learning about your sales cycle and hit rate. Let's talk about these measurements.

Your *sales cycle* is defined as the average time it takes for a prospect to commit to your project or buy your product from the time he or she was first introduced to it. Sometimes, your sales cycle can be immediate. If you have books for sale at the back of the room, you can expect participants to make instantaneous decisions about buying a book. Purchasing your products or services may require more extensive decisionmaking, which means your sales cycle could range from a few weeks to many months.

Knowing your sales cycle will help you plan future seminars. You can plan a seminar with a realistic estimate of attaining a certain number of leads and can calculate how long it takes people to make up their minds. This information

SAMPLE #4
BUDGET

Item	Budget	Actual
Office overhead		
Telephone		
Secretarial		
Photocopying		
Marketing		
Advertisements		
Invitations		
Brochures		
Postage		
Venue		
Room rental		
Coat check		
Parking		
Signs		
Gratuities (serving staff, hotel employees)		
Taxes		
Food and beverage		
Presentation		
Audiovisual equipment		
Handout material		
Speaker's fees		
Speaker's expenses		
Guests		
Name tags, tent cards		
On-site staff		
Gifts		
Door prizes		
Other		

can be tremendously helpful for your future business planning and the planning of your prospecting seminar schedule.

Your *hit rate* is the number of prospects that turn into business. By tracking your leads from each seminar carefully, you will find that not all leads result in commitments. Your hit rate is only those leads that actually turn into business. Knowing your hit rate will help you determine if the number of attendees you are inviting and the amount of money you are spending really makes sense in terms of helping your overall bottom line.

One final word, remember to pay all your bills on time: you may want to use that facility again.

m. IT'S SHOW TIME

You must remember one crucial rule the day of your seminar: arrive early! Remember Murphy's Law: anything that can go wrong will go wrong. So arrive early and expect to have to do everything yourself. Consider anything done in advance as a welcome surprise.

By communicating carefully with the facility's sales and catering departments before the seminar, you will cut down on problems, but you will not eliminate them. When you arrive on-site the day of the seminar, bring all your paperwork pertaining to the site, including the name of the person you spoke with from each department and what you ordered.

Remember to pack an emergency kit containing office supplies including pens, paper, stapler, paper clips, felt markers, change for the telephone, business cards, extra handout materials, and anything else you think you will need. You can't rely on the facility to have these available.

If a problem does arise, stay calm and professional. In fact, unless the problem is catastrophic, your audience may not even notice — if you remain calm and don't panic.

The planning master checklist on the next page includes a list of things you must check on before your guests arrive.

n. AFTER IT'S OVER

All your planning has reaped its rewards. Your seminar has been a success, but your work is not finished. Now is the time to implement your follow-up strategy. Set aside time so that you can contact within seven days of the seminar everyone who attended. See chapter 9 for a full discussion on follow-up strategies.

SEMINAR PLANNING MASTER CHECKLIST

Assign roles and responsibilities ☐

Select your seminar topic ☐

Choose a speaker if necessary ☐

Choose a time for your seminar ☐

Site inspection: choosing the right site

    Accessible location ☐

    Affordable (check optional sites) ☐

    Transportation ☐

    Special needs facilities ☐

    Elevators ☐

    Parking ☐

    Handicapped access ☐

    Washrooms ☐

    Coat check ☐

    Telephones ☐

    Security ☐

    Catering ☐

    General cleanliness ☐

    Renovations in progress or planned ☐

Room location ☐

    Noise, smell, neighbors ☐

Business service center ☐

Negotiate a contract ☐

Confirm everything in writing ☐

Get map ☐

Establish credit ☐

Room inspection

Room size ☐

Space for podium and/or stage ☐

Space for audiovisual equipment ☐

Pillars arranged so not blocking
audience's view ☐

Ceiling height ☐

Lighting ☐

Light and heat controls ☐

Room setup

Registration area: two tables ☐

Number of chairs ☐

Extra chairs available ☐

Setup options (seating plan sent in advance) ☐

Information table ☐

Speaker's table ☐

Music ☐

Decorations ☐

Food and beverage

Time to serve ☐

What to serve ☐

Dietary considerations ☐

Preregistration

Mail ☐

Telephone ☐

Fax ☐

E-mail ☐

Staff to take registrations ☐

Preregistration procedures ☐

Registration forms ☐

Confirmation letters ☐

Signage

Directional signs ☐

Registration signs ☐

Welcome sign ☐

Sponsor signs ☐

Presentation tools

    Check equipment suppliers ☐

    On-site ☐

    Screen angle ☐

    Taped wires ☐

    Sound check ☐

    Spare bulbs ☐

Handout material

    Develop ☐

    Distribute ☐

    Name badges ☐

    Blank name badges ☐

    Collateral materials ☐

    Workshop notes ☐

    Evaluation forms ☐

Last-minute check on day of seminar

    Front board lists your meeting correctly ☐

    Directional signs in place ☐

    Room is set up as ordered ☐

    Extra chairs available in adjacent room ☐

    Microphone is working at proper level ☐

    Overhead projector properly focused ☐

Slide projector focused and remote control in the forward position ☐

VCR cued ☐

Flip chart has enough paper and markers are working ☐

Room temperature comfortable ☐

Light switch adjustments working to dim the room ☐

You know the locations of washrooms and telephones ☐

Refreshments ready ☐

Catering staff know when they can enter the room to set up or clear ☐

Hotel operators aware of your meeting so they can accept last-minute calls. ☐

Ringer turned off the house telephone ☐

Coat racks have enough hangers for all your guests' coats ☐

Registration table set up with the name badges for each participant who pre-registered, as well as blanks to be filled in by walk-in guests ☐

Review evaluations and do follow-up ☐

4
MARKETING: SPREADING THE WORD

What if you planned a seminar and nobody came? Sounds like a devastating scenario, but it could happen if you do not entice people to your event.

Marketing your seminar is probably the most important stage in your planning activities. It will help you eliminate the risk of failure. Without a good marketing plan, nothing else happens. Your job is to sell your seminar to your target audience, and with so many seminars to choose from and the time pressure most people now feel, you have to provide something new and different if you are going to get people out to your event.

These days, you are competing against so many other forms of entertainment. Instead of going to your seminar, your potential guests may choose to attend a movie, sporting event, political rally, or parents' association meeting. To get them to see *you*, you are going to have to make it worth their while.

a. GETTING FOCUSED

To develop a winning marketing plan, you need to focus on your target market, the marketing options available to you, and the tools to implement these options.

First, consider your audience. You have targeted your seminar at a particular group based on a fundamental grasp of their wants and needs. Before proceeding further, you must understand your audience in greater depth so that you are able to choose marketing tools that will most likely appeal to it. Audience preferences can be determined by examining and understanding the *demographics* and *psychographics* of your audience.

Demographics include age, sex, income, buying patterns, family size, household size, education, occupation, geographic location, marital status, and family makeup. The demographics of your targeted audience members offer you a first look at who they are. This information will help significantly in your seminar planning. Everything from your choice of topic to the choice of venue will be affected by demographics.

But knowing this basic information merely opens the door. Taking it one step further provides you with even greater benefits. While demographics tell you *who* you are dealing with, psychographics tell you *what* motivates them. Psychographics describe what your target audience members care about, how they feel about issues, what they value, and how they choose to live their lives. Such insights into what motivates them provide information you can use to fine-tune your seminar marketing. Look at their activities such as work, hobbies, vacation and entertainment choices, lifestyle (family, home, recreation, community), and their opinions on self-image, social issues, education, health, and the future.

Your understanding of this information not only ensures that your seminar is well targeted but it also addresses important details such as the food you serve, the topic and speaker you choose, and the time you choose for the seminar. You can market and plan your seminar to complement your audience's values and interests.

How your target audience responds to information also affects the timing of your promotion. Start your promotion early, about six to ten weeks ahead for people who are long-range planners, slow decision makers, and those who have a full schedule. For people who act more on impulse, two to five weeks is a good lead time.

You can find demographic and psychographic information at your local library. Government statistics can be helpful, and there may be available surveys or research reports published by local newspapers, magazines, and television or radio stations, as well as by community or consumer groups.

b. YOUR MARKETING OPTIONS

Once you have a clear understanding of the demographics and psychographics of your audience, you are ready to check out your marketing options. Finding the right marketing mix is limited only by your creativity. You might choose to promote your seminars at trade shows, use paid advertising on radio or television, solicit editorial coverage in the newspapers — the list is endless. There is no right or wrong way; just remember to use your demographic and psychographic information to find the best marketing mix for you. For example, you need to research which newspapers and magazines the members of your target audience read if you want to focus on print advertising and editorial coverage.

Use the list of ideas in the rest of this section to create a marketing plan using the techniques you feel will work best for you. Before acting on any of these marketing options, make sure they meet some basic criteria. Use the acronym ACT to help you decide what will work best for you. ACT stands for *availability, cost,* and *timing.* These are the three elements that will keep you on track. When you compare each marketing option using these elements, some will stand out as viable options and others will be an obvious waste of your time and energy.

1. Cooperative marketing

(a) Availability

Marketing your seminar through a partnership with another organization is a great way to increase your audience. Chambers of commerce, professional associations, or boards of trade often look for activities that will bring added value to their members.

(b) Cost

Generally, the cost of partnering is in cross-promotional activities rather than in cash. Partners look for exposure. They ask for their name on your marketing pieces (for example, "In cooperation with . . ."), or they may want to set up a table or do some of their own promotion at your seminar. In return, they may offer you an opportunity to make a presentation at one of their meetings, place signs for the seminars in their meeting areas, or give you advertising space in their newsletters.

(c) Timing

Professional organizations usually plan well ahead and often have an agenda of activities spanning six to eight months. There may not be room for last-minute additions. If you choose to market through partnerships, make sure you plan well in advance. If the timing of their meetings fits into your seminar plans, great. If there is a conflict: beware.

I discuss partnerships in more detail in the next chapter.

2. Trade shows

(a) Availability

Trade shows are the granddaddy of marketing events and are an excellent way to market your products and services; they are where large groups of people congregate for a short period. Exhibitors are at trade shows to look for business leads or to support their marketing plans.

Trade shows are also a great place to recruit people to attend your seminars. Trade shows are plentiful; consider participating in local business shows, seniors' shows, parent shows, travel and leisure shows, fall fairs, and investment shows.

Directories listing shows by subject, geography, and time are available at your local library. You can also find upcoming shows by consulting show facilities.

(b) Cost

The cost of exhibiting can be high. You will have to pay for · space rental, booth hardware, promotion, and your time.

(c) Timing

Trade shows are scheduled at least a year in advance, and each generally takes place at the same time each year. If you plan to use trade shows to promote a seminar, your seminar schedule will have to be set to coincide with the show.

3. Radio: paid advertising

(a) Availability

Buying radio time is easy. You need to study the various stations in your area and pick the times you feel are best suited to reach your target audience. Ask each station you are considering to furnish you with a copy of their ratings.

Radio stations commission independent companies to survey listeners to determine what they listen to and what they want to listen to. These ratings help station managers formulate programing for the upcoming period. You can get copies of these reports if you ask for them. In the United States, this information is provided by Nielsen or Arbitron. In Canada, such reports are available from the Canadian Bureau of Broadcasters or the Bureau of Broadcaster Management.

By studying rating reports, you will learn which radio station most appeals to members of your target audience, which shows they listen to, when they listen, and which radio personalities they relate to most. All this information is extremely important when you have a choice of stations on which spend your advertising dollars.

(b) Cost

The cost of radio advertising depends on the time of the air play. Obviously, the times when the most listeners are tuned-in will be the most expensive. A 30-second radio spot can run from $30 to $300 depending on the time of day and frequency of your advertising.

In his book *The Do-it-Yourself Business Promotions Kit,* Jack Griffin talks about the effectiveness of advertising during drive times versus nondrive times. Typically, the morning drive time is from 6:00 a.m. to 10:00 a.m., and the afternoon drive time is from 3:00 p.m. to 7:00 p.m. In large metropolitan areas where there are many commuters, many people will be sitting in their cars listening to the radio during the two daily drive times. In a smaller community where people spend less time in their cars, drive time is of less importance to effective advertising.

Aside from drive time, you have a number of options to examine. Some stations run public service announcements. Some will work with you on a per-inquiry payment option (i.e., you pay a certain amount for each telephone inquiry resulting from your ad). Others will negotiate a price based on the number of announcements and the time of day they run.

Further options include ROS (run of station), where the station decides when the spot is to be run; BTA (best time available), where the station will allocate your spots in order of your most desirable time, running in descending order to your least desirable time); and TAP (total audience plan), where you dictate the exact time you want your spots to run. Each option will be priced differently.

You may be able to negotiate lower rates for multiple advertising, by advertising in slower times, or by taking advantage of station specials.

(c) Timing

To be effective, consider running your radio spot a number of times. Running it only once is usually ineffective.

4. Radio: editorial coverage

(a) Availability

Many seminars are marketed on the radio. The station manager can direct you to the program that will help you best reach your audience. You have several options to consider. From the office listener, the commuter, the early riser, or the late-night listener, there is a suitable time slot for you.

Both local AM and FM broadcast bands have some programming covering local interests. These programs take the form of a regular talk-radio segment or a current-events program. Often, government regulations require radio stations to give some time to local initiatives. However, stations shy away from those that are strictly profit oriented. Many radio stations have talk shows that are always looking for exciting new guests.

Offer to do a call-in show in the field of your expertise. You will be able to mention that your upcoming seminar will give listeners more information. The trick is not to make any discussion of your seminar sound like a pitch.

Listen carefully to the various stations to get an idea of their content. Speak to the producers of the shows you think may be interested in having you as a guest. You will need to give them a hook that will appeal to their listeners. With a little research and some perseverance, radio can be a great method of promoting your seminar.

Keep in mind that you cannot put all your hopes on the results of editorial coverage on radio. Since the producers of these shows are keenly interested in programming that is timely, you run the risk of being bumped at the last minute if a more time-sensitive story is available.

(b) Cost

Radio editorial is free. However, you must consider the time and effort you put into researching, preparing a written proposal, following up with the program producers, and then preparing for the show.

(c) Timing

Timing is critical. You want to give the producers a lot of notice, but if you start too early, they will be immersed in more current issues and may not give your proposal the time it deserves. Remember, you can't count on radio editorial, but if successful, it can be an excellent addition to your overall seminar marketing.

5. Television: paid advertising

(a) Availability

Television is changing rapidly. With the introduction of specialized stations on cable and satellite, the number of television advertising options have expanded significantly beyond the traditional networks. These cable and satellite networks offer you a variety of specialized channels, such as a real estate channel, a shopping channel, and a weather channel. Some also run a television-listing channel where a banner or a message on a split screen is used for advertising.

(b) Cost

According to conventional wisdom, television advertising is expensive. This is true when you compare the cost of national television coverage with other forms of national advertising, but at the local level, you have some affordable options.

On cable, your advertisement may consist of on-screen text with a professional announcer or background music. The listing will roll throughout the broadcast time. Alternatively, you may purchase 15-, 30- or 60-second spots on a predetermined airing schedule. Some cable networks will guarantee exposure at least 12 times each day, costing from $200 to $500 per week for a minimum time, somewhere between 6 and 12 weeks.

(c) Timing

Although they will try their best, cable stations will not guarantee to give you the exact time you request your advertisement be run. While television is often considered the sexy form of advertising, there are some time limitations. You need to allow time to prepare the proper text, choose the right announcer, and if the commercial is to include some drama, the additional time and expense of the shoot. Advertising on television can provide very powerful exposure, but it is not a last-minute marketing solution, so give yourself lots of time to prepare.

6. Television: editorial coverage

(a) Availability

Television provides many good editorial opportunities. In your community, there may be many shows that are locally produced and of local interest. While you may dream of being on *Oprah,* such exposure is likely beyond the scope of your seminar.

Spend some time reviewing the television listings and watching the programing that is produced locally both on cable and on network stations. If you think your story is suited to a particular program, watch the credits at the end of the program to find the name of the show producer, or simply call the station and ask for the producer's name. Send the producer your press release and be prepared to follow up regularly.

(b) Cost

The cost of television editorial coverage is minimal. It requires a good media release and time spent researching and following up.

(c) Timing

If your seminar topic is related to something that is going on in your community, you stand a good chance of exposure.

However, this form of marketing is highly unreliable since, as with radio editorial coverage, you are subject to being bumped by more timely, late-breaking stories.

7. Print: paid advertising

(a) Availability

You have many print options, including newspapers, magazines, and newsletters. Newspaper advertisements appeal to the general public and work well for a broad audience. If your community has more than one daily newspaper, you need to do some research to decide in which paper to advertise. Find out the editorial focus of the paper, its rates, deadlines, and circulation, as well as information on its readership.

What options do you have for the placement of your advertisement? Do you want to be in the front section, the arts, real estate, family, business, or financial section?

Find out whether you could list your seminar in a section about community news or with the public service announcements. Many papers have free weekly business and events calendars. Keep a record of the publication deadlines for these calendars.

Also take a look at publications such as trade journals and association newsletters, which target special interest groups. As well as reaching your target audience, these publications have a longer shelf life than daily or weekly newspapers and you will get multiple hits as the publications are usually passed on to several people.

(b) Cost

Print advertisements are usually charged by the agate line. Fourteen agate lines equals one inch times the width of the column. Each newspaper has different column widths, so you need to ask about this when you are comparing rates. Ask your account representative for a media kit, which will include rates, demographics, and sample advertisements.

Advertisements in magazines are usually based on page size. You can purchase a whole, half, quarter, eighth, or sixteenth of a page, or a business-card size. Once again, you should ask for media kits so you can compare magazine to magazine.

(c) Timing

Whether they are daily, weekly, or monthly, magazines and newspapers are published on regular schedules. It is important to place multiple advertisements if you choose to advertise in a daily. Also, you do not want your advertisement to appear too far in advance. You should start newspaper advertisements two to three weeks before your event. All publications have strict deadlines; ask the account representative what they are and plan accordingly.

8. Print: editorial coverage

(a) Availability

Editorial options in the print medium include interviews with local journalists, letters to the editor, and articles that you write and can persuade someone to publish.

Newsworthy items are always welcome if they are of interest to the community, but you will seldom get space if your story appears to be for profit. This means that your media release should focus on how your seminar will be tackling issues relevant to the community.

(b) Cost

There is no direct cost for editorial coverage in print other than the time you spend researching and writing.

(c) Timing

Print editorial is a very powerful marketing option. The risk, as in radio and television, is that no one at the publication can guarantee when your story will run. However, print editorial coverage is well worth chasing as a backup to your paid marketing.

9. Direct mail

(a) Availability

You may be thinking that unsolicited mail is nothing more than junk mail. However, if it is properly constructed, it is a highly effective marketing option and the most popular method of promoting seminars. The huge advantage of direct mail is that it can be targeted directly to those people you have identified as potential seminar participants through your demographic and pyschographic research.

Start by using your own mailing list, which gives you an opportunity to make contact with clients and friends. If handled properly, your clients will appreciate receiving new information from you, and if you ask, they will usually pass it along to others they feel will benefit from it.

For a larger mailing, consider contacting a list broker. You can find list brokers listed in the Yellow Pages under "Mailing lists." These companies specialize in direct mail and have lists that you can purchase or rent. Brokers will work with many list owners to compile your list. There are all kinds of consumer lists, and if you have a well-focused target audience, a list broker can put together a customized mailing for your seminar. Ask the broker how lists are updated and how data are verified.

List brokers estimate that a good rate of return on a direct-mail campaign is 2%, although tightly targeted lists can produce up to a 20% response rate. The response rate depends on the quality of the list and how targeted it is, the timing, and the quality of your marketing piece. To increase your response rate, use first-class postage and add an incentive, time limit, or offer of a free gift for attending your seminar.

Many books are available that can help you develop an effective direct-mail piece. Take the time to put together an attention-grabbing item that will reap you rewards.

(b) Cost

List brokers charge by list size. They will either give you names on labels or on a diskette for a one-time mailing, or, more typically, they will arrange the mailing on your behalf. When working with list brokers, ask if they provide guarantees on the delivery rates of their lists. A 10% mis-mail rate is an industry average. Ask for a refund of a portion of the mail costs if the volume returned is too high.

Costs will vary. Very basic business-to-business lists are taken from standard sources such as telephone books, industrial directories, and government agency lists. Although these are less expensive, they are not as reliable as lists compiled from more targeted sources. These lists can start at $75 per 1,000 names, with additional charges for each criterion you add.

Many list brokers have a minimum, for example, 5,000 names for $800 or $900. So unless you plan to do a very extensive mailing, it may be not suitable for you to use these list brokers.

Many associations rent lists. Consider the associations your target audience may belong to and approach them to purchase their lists. Some provide labels or a diskette while others do the mailing for you for an extra fee. These lists are typically for one-time use only.

Some organizations will give you their lists for free if they believe in your program and if it will provide valuable information to their members. These organizations may ask for a role in your seminar in return for the list. In some cases, they may do a dedicated mailing and charge you for the postage only. However, more often, they will include your direct-mail piece in a prearranged mailing. Before they commit to include your piece in their mailings, they will need to see the piece to confirm its size and weight and the suitability of the content.

A word of caution: do not use membership lists without permission. Many associations promise their members there will be no solicitation without the blessing of the board. You can cause a lot of ill-will toward your seminar by using lists without authorization.

If you have hired guest speakers, ask them if they are willing to let you use their mailing lists for the event. They may provide you with the list for a one-time use or even do a mailing themselves.

The standard equation used by many direct-mail marketers to measure results is promotion cost divided by number of responses equals cost per response:

$$\frac{\text{promotion cost}}{\text{number of responses}} = \text{cost per response}$$

For more information on direct mail, contact the Direct Marketing Association in New York City at (212) 768-7277 or visit its Web site at *www.dma.org.* In Canada, contact the Canadian Direct Marketing Association in Toronto at (416) 391-2362 or visit its Web site at *www.cdma.org.* Also, a very useful reference in Canada is *CARD (Canadian Advertising Rates and Data Directory).* It is published monthly by Maclean Hunter Publishing in Toronto. Check out the Web site at *www.cardmedia.com.* In the United States, contact *Direct Mail List Rates and Data,* published by Standard Rate and Data Services.

(c) Timing

Direct mail is the most flexible of all the marketing methods in terms of timing. You can usually organize your mailing to coincide specifically with your seminar. When you work with associations, however, you may lose some of this flexibility because their mailings are often sent on a predetermined schedule.

10. The Internet

(a) Availability

The Internet has become an increasingly popular marketing option. Like the fax machine and the telephone before it, the Internet is fast becoming an essential communication tool for business.

The Internet is the electronic equivalent to a global toll-free number. Yet, while global in scope, it has tremendous applications on a local level. The Internet can help you reach and service your customers, and because it is interactive, it enhances the communication between you and your customers.

To do business on the Internet, you will need to develop a Web site. This is not an easy task if you lack some of the basic computer skills needed. Find a Web site developer who can help you ensure access to your local audience. Your Web site designer can build codes into your program so that your site will come up when there is an enquiry specific to your location and services. For example, someone looking for a seminar on financial planning might type in "seminar, Seattle, financial planning" and your site will come up. For more information on building your own Web site, see *Winning Web Sites*, published by Self-Counsel Press.

The Internet can be a great help to you in marketing your seminar. Follow the advice of Brian Hurley and Peter Birkwood in their book *Doing Big Business on the Internet*, also published by Self-Counsel Press. They suggest you ask yourself these questions before putting your business on the Internet:

(a) Is your seminar a natural fit to the Internet environment? The Internet environment is a faceless transaction between you and the prospect. If it is necessary for members of your target audience to develop a feeling of trust before they attend a seminar, you need to design your site to reflect this. Be sure that you establish your credibility.

(b) Is your target market on the Internet? There is no point to marketing on the Internet if your market doesn't have access to it. Check the demographics of your target market carefully to ensure that it is computer friendly. Find out from your local Internet service provider (ISP) who, in demographic terms, has enrolled in its service. And don't make assumptions about people based on their age or ability; there is a growing acceptance of the computer and the Internet. Even seniors who were born well before the information age began are becoming computer literate.

The Internet also provides opportunities through newsgroups and e-mail. You may wish to get involved in a newsgroup to help spread the word about your seminar. Each ISP has its own newsgroups to which you can subscribe. Find a newsgroup that you believe will be interested in your products or services, and in your seminar. Spend some time on the Internet with the different newsgroups to get a flavor of what they are about before posting anything.

Once you have identified a newsgroup that you feel is well matched to your business, prepare a short note about your service and seminar and post it. Make sure that you are offering valuable information to attract and keep newsgroup participants or they will easily tire. Keep your message short, and try to make it not sound commercial. People become upset if newsgroup members post advertisements. Offer them something that will whet their appetite for more.

E-mail allows customers to communicate with you after normal business hours and eliminates telephone tag. You can acquire e-mail lists through one of the many search engines on the Internet. Some ISPs offer a service that creates an e-mail list based on your criteria. They can also complete the transmission for you.

As you develop your Internet marketing options, keep in mind that your Internet identity must be easy to contact and must be memorable. Develop an easy-to-remember Internet address. Try to have the name impart something about your services, so that people surfing the Internet on those subjects will come across your site. Include your Web site and e-mail address on everything: on your business cards, stationery, invoices, labels, promotional pieces, and all advertising.

(b) Cost

Advertising on a popular Web site can be very expensive. However, there are ways to reduce the cost and still target your audience. Rena Amer of Add Value International in Mississauga, Canada, suggests contacting a supplier related to your seminar topic to purchase a banner advertisement on its Web site. The fee for this is considerably less than it would cost you to create your own Web site.

(c) Timing

It is not worthwhile to put up a Web site that has only short-term value. Your Internet marketing should be a long-term commitment. If people get used to finding your site on the Internet, they are more likely to respond. Create a dynamic site, and change it regularly to keep it fresh and appealing.

11. Public relations

(a) Availability

Public relations includes all those things that are not directly paid for. Press conferences, talk shows, newspaper stories, listings in local business calendars, and public service announcements are just a few examples of these activities. Getting good public relations is not as easy as it may seem.

Everyone is looking for his or her 15 minutes of fame. The media are constantly inundated with requests for coverage.

(b) Cost

You can drum up public relations yourself or you can hire a public relations firm to do it for you. Many good media contacts can be found through your networking activities. However, the value of a professional firm is that it has already nurtured these contacts and can advise you on whom to approach and when to approach them. They can also help you develop your media release and make sure that it will grab the attention of your targeted media.

Public relations firms usually charge by the hour though you may be able to negotiate a fixed-price contract. Whether you solicit the media yourself or have someone else do so, there is always the risk that there will be no interest in your story.

(c) Timing

Timing your public relations is very difficult. Public relations is an ongoing activity that needs to be nurtured. Keep in touch with your contacts regularly — whether you send them new stories or just a quick note about something they may be interested in. Again, you always run the risk of having your story bumped if a more timely or more newsworthy story comes up. Often, even the media have little or no control over these interruptions.

12. Networking

(a) Availability

Many of us fail to think of networking as a viable marketing option. Yet, "networking is an activity with real purpose, plan, and outcome. Networking is your ability to get out of your comfortable work environment and meet new people who will enhance your business," says Barry Siskind, author of *Making Contact* published by Macmillan Canada. "These people and their colleagues can form the basis of your seminar audience. The trick to good networking is choosing the right places to network. It requires a real understanding of what the various venues offer you and who their audience is. If their audience is also yours, there is a match."

(b) Cost

The cost of networking is minimal. It can include the membership fees you have to pay to belong to organizations and associations, or the luncheon or event fees that are often attached to specific events. But networking opportunities are found everywhere, from the health club locker room to a church or parents' group. It is all a matter of tuning in your business antenna to seek out opportunities.

(c) Timing

Networking is an ongoing business task. To build your business in the first place, you needed contacts along the way. Now that you are promoting a specific event, it is important to go back to those contacts and entice them to come to your seminar.

13. Word-of-mouth marketing

(a) Availability

There is no one as talkative as a happy customer. It has often been said that word-of-mouth marketing can make or break an event. The movie industry provides a great example of this theory. We have all seen big-budget movies come out with a great splash, then quickly fade into oblivion. Word-of-mouth marketing is directly related to quality. If the quality of the movie lives up to the expectations of theater-goers and critics, their comments will be positive.

The same holds true for your seminar. Your reputation will precede you. If you are known in a community as a hard-working, ethical businessperson, you can be sure that your clients will be talking about your business attributes. If you have held successful seminars in the past, you can count on previous attendees to help spread the word.

(b) Cost

The cost of marketing by word-of-mouth is simply the cost of doing good business: providing attentive service, quality products, and constant customer care. Beyond that, there is no cost.

(c) Timing

If you want to take advantage of word-of-mouth marketing, time your next seminar so that you are able to mention it to your current participants. If they were pleased with the seminar they just attended, ask them to pass the word on about your next seminar to their friends and colleagues.

Alternatively, if you do not have another seminar booked yet, ask participants for names of people who they think would benefit from the seminar, and add these names to your mailing list.

14. Telemarketing

(a) Availability

I doubt that anyone reading this book has ever escaped being called by a telemarketer at one time or another. People's reactions to telemarketers are sometimes positive, sometimes negative, yet telemarketing is still around. Why? Because it works.

Telemarketing is more than simply calling a stranger to solicit a charitable donation, offer to clean carpets, or sell printing supplies. If conducted professionally, telemarketing can be a very effective way of reaching your target audience in person.

(b) Cost

You can pay a telemarketer on an hourly basis, per call, or per reservation. It all depends on your level of confidence in the person who is doing it. In addition to the telemarketer's telephone time, you will also have to spend some time working with him or her to develop a focused script.

If you have the time, consider making the calls yourself. Nobody knows your market and seminar plans better than you. And doing it yourself is more than a cost-saving device: it also lets you reach out to your audience directly. As you are talking to possible participants, you have a chance to learn more about them and begin to develop rapport.

(c) Timing

The beauty of telemarketing is that you can do it whenever it is appropriate. You have complete control over the timing. If you choose to do it yourself, you need to allow for time in your busy schedule. Put aside a certain number of hours each day to make cold calls. This kind of disciplined approach can yield great rewards.

15. Fax broadcasting

(a) Availability

Move over junk mail, now we have junk fax. Unless it is handled properly, your fax contact with prospective guests will receive no more consideration than any other unsolicited announcement. But if you do it properly, fax technology can yield huge rewards.

A fax broadcast is just what the name implies: the sending of faxes to a large number of people in a short period. Properly planned, you can reach hundreds of people overnight. For large-volume seminars, you may want to consider fax-on-demand and fax-back services, which will speed up your response to your prospect but will also eliminate personal contact.

(b) Cost

You can buy software to set up your own fax broadcasting system or you can use the services of a professional company.

The cost will depend on the length of your broadcast and the number of prospects you are sending to but is substantially lower than direct mail. Cathy Reed, vice president of International Teledata Group, offers this comparison: To send 2 pages to 500 prospects across Canada by direct mail will take 40 hours to prepare, 3 days to deliver, and cost $1,325 in postage and labor. The same "mailing" by fax broadcast would take 1 hour to prepare, 1 hour to deliver, and $400 in broadcast costs.

(c) Timing

Fax broadcasts are not limited by postal delays. You can use the fax to send initial announcements about your seminar or to send a last-minute reminder to those who have expressed interest but who have still not registered. You have complete control of timing.

c. MARKETING TOOLS

1. Media release

If you want to get media attention, you will have to use the tools the media are most familiar with. The media, particularly in large metropolitan centers, are overwhelmed with solicitations for attention. Weeding through all the requests becomes an impossible task. To give yourself the best chance, you need to develop a good media release.

A media release is a one-page document intended to get an editor's attention. Although there are some basics that you need to understand about media releases, much of what you do is up to you. Remember, the easier you make the editor's job, the better your chances are of success.

(a) The hook

Editors will consider your release if you offer something that will interest their readers. Their priority is to find newsworthy stories, not to promote your seminar. Avoid media releases that smack of commercialism. A good rule is to first read the various publications to which you plan to send your media release and determine the slant of their stories. If you are running a real estate seminar for example, telling the editor that his or her readers will learn how to successfully invest in real estate will probably not raise much excitement. But captions such as "Learn the secrets of millionaires" or "Make money in a recession!" might be a stronger hook.

Different editors will look for different angles. A business editor will be attracted to money-making or money-saving ideas. An entertainment editor will be interested in the arts, and a lifestyles editor will be interested in things that affect the way people live. This means your hook not only has to be targeted for the publication but also for the specific section within a publication.

Editors are overwhelmed with information each day. There has to be a compelling reason for them to read your media release.

(b) The body

In the body of the media release, you have a chance to expand on the hook. Here you will take the theme you have created and give the editor more substance. In fact, you are outlining the story for the editor. The body of the piece need only be a few short paragraphs and be something like:

> **Learn the secrets of millionaires**
> Behind every fabulously wealthy family lies a solid real estate portfolio. The Rockefellers, Kennedys, and Bronfmans all boast some of the best real estate in the world. Through good times and bad, the heirs of these families continue to live lavish lifestyles, thanks to the shrewd investments made by their ancestors. Is the wealth in real estate limited to these few families? Certainly not.

In one short weekend, our participants will learn the secrets to building their own real estate empire from successful investors who for the first time are willing to share their secrets. Your readers will learn how to avoid the six pitfalls most commonly associated with real estate investments (remember the Reichmanns), the five best emerging markets, and a step-by-step guide which will put them on the road to financial freedom.

(c) The close

In the close, you need to tell the editor where, when, why, who, and how the publication's readers can get involved. For example:

Where: Holiday Inn

When: October 31, 7:00 p.m.

Why: This is the first time this seminar has been available to people in our community

Who: Conducted by the Get Rich Real Estate Company and master investor J.R. Moneybags

How: Available by calling 1-800-GET-RICH

Before sending your media release, find out the name of the editor to direct it to. After sending your media release, make a follow-up telephone call to ensure the editor has received it. More times than not, he or she will not have seen it and you will need to send it again.

The editorial and advertising departments in most publications are separate and do not influence each other. However, a well-placed advertisement will be more powerful if it is in the same edition as your editorial. If you plan to place ads, try to coordinate them with an editorial.

2. Brochure or marketing piece

Remember the expression, "You only get one chance to make a first impression"? This holds particularly true when referring to your marketing piece. When you send something in the mail, it has to make a strong first impression, which means that it gets recipients' attention quickly so they will spend a few minutes reading it.

It's important to take great care when creating your marketing piece. There are companies that can help you develop marketing materials or you can do it yourself. If you have good writing skills, basic word-processing skills, a creative flair, and an understanding of what attracts people's attention quickly, you have the basic ingredients necessary to do the job yourself. If you lack some of these skills or just don't feel comfortable trying to create the marketing piece yourself, find a professional to help you.

Your marketing piece is what spreads the word about your seminar. There are many places beyond the mail you can use it, for example, at trade shows or mall exhibits, as handouts at community activities or chamber of commerce meetings — anywhere you network.

If you are holding more than one seminar, you can realize some economies of scale by listing multiple dates and locations on one brochure.

(a) Headline

Your brochure has to grab readers' attention in the first few seconds. This happens with a strong eye-catching headline:

Never lose another night's sleep!
Goodbye thinning hair!
Invest in emerging markets!
Learn the secrets of the most successful people!
One million people can't be wrong!

(b) The benefits

The wording of your brochure should stress the benefits people will receive by attending your seminar. Tell people what they will get. How it will change them? What's in it for them?

Keep this information very simple, using just two or three central points. Your message should be practical and specific:

By attending this seminar, you will learn:
The seven steps to financial security
How to avoid the five most common pitfalls
Develop a plan you and your family can live with

(c) Photographs

A picture is worth a thousand slogans. Use pictures or drawings to reinforce your benefit statement. If you are planning a retirement seminar, your brochure might have a picture of a golfer playing on a beautifully manicured golf course. Or if you are talking about health alternatives, use photographs of active people who look bright and happy.

Use one primary visual rather than many photographs. Use big, bold print, easy-to read type, lots of white space, and short, reader-friendly sentences.

(d) Testimonials

Testimonials from past participants increase your credibility. Before you use testimonials, be sure to get permission to do so from the writers.

(e) The presenter

Include a bit about the presenter with a photo to make the person seem real. This can help build rapport as your potential attendees, seeing the picture, feel they have already met the person.

(f) Take-away materials

Mention what participants will take away with them from the seminar, such as handouts, planning sheets, or samples.

(g) Color

You want your brochure to stand out from other marketing pieces your prospective participant receives. Color can be tied into the overall theme of your seminar or it can stand on its own. For example, if your seminar has some connection to environmental issues, using green paper or ink might be appropriate. If you are speaking on very serious topics, such as funeral planning, using dark colors may be appropriate.

(h) Call for action

Tell people how they can register. Provide telephone and fax numbers, as well as your e-mail address. Refer to your Web site if you have one. Make contacting you as easy as possible for prospective participants. Keep in mind, though, that offering too many options or choices can lead to confusion and people might just ignore the offer to register.

3. Advertisements

Designing your advertisement is similar to designing your marketing piece. You need to attract readers' attention quickly with a compelling headline. Describe your seminar and tell them why they should attend.

The difference between a marketing piece and an advertisement is space. In a marketing piece, you have space for a lot of information. In an advertisement, you are limited because space equals money. Your message needs to be brief and efficient.

The layout for your advertisement should include the basic information you put into your marketing brochure, but in a condensed version. Include the benefits of attending, what participants will learn, information about the presenter, a photo or sketch, and a description of the registration procedure.

If you have the budget, you may also want to consider a teaser advertisement. This is a small advertisement placed several times in a publication to pique the curiosity of your audience. This type of advertisement consists of a headline, telephone number, and very short description.

4. Posters

If you live in a large metropolitan area, you undoubtedly will have noticed telephone posts, boarding around construction sites, and bus stop shelters plastered with posters promoting rock concerts, plays, books, and religious revival meetings. You can picture a promoter hiring legions of hourly paid workers, giving them lots of paste, and setting them loose on an unsuspecting city.

This is the extreme of postering. Although many municipalities object to this type of marketing, posters are still effective if they are displayed discreetly. If your seminar has an emotional appeal, preparing posters can be a very useful way of drawing an audience. Posters can be placed in locations that your audience will visit, such as libraries, community centers, hospitals, daycare centers, and municipal offices. Always obtain permission to put up your posters from the appropriate authorities.

If you have a sponsor for your seminar (see chapter 5), your distribution of posters can be much wider. For example, you might place posters in every quick-copy shop or in the foyers of banks or trust companies.

The poster needs a strong headline, an appealing picture, some sharp copy, and a call to action. As with the brochure, you may want to have a professional design your poster.

5. Invitations

Think back to when you were a kid and received an invitation to a friend's birthday party. The invitation likely looked like this:

> You are invited to Billy's birthday party
> Date and time: October 31 at 5:00 p.m.
> Place: Billy's house
> Theme: Wear your Halloween costume
> Have your parents pick you up at 8:00 p.m.
> once the party ends
> *RSVP: 555-6780*

This basic invitation is similar to the invitation you might send to prospective seminar guests. Like Billy's, your invitation answers the five Ws: Who, What, When, Where, and Why. However, unlike Billy's invitation, yours will need to be a bit more informative. You have to give people a compelling reason to attend your seminar.

The look of your invitations can vary. You are limited only by your good taste and imagination. Your invitation can take the form of a letter, postcard, pop-up card, or formal fold-over. You can send it in a bottle, special wrapping, or courier pack. Consider including other fun items that tie into the theme of your seminar, such as a golf ball, letter opener, pack of coffee or tea bag and mug, facsimile of a $100 bill, model car (Mercedes or Rolls Royce), or anything else you can think of that will capture people's imagination.

Your invitation should include all the basic information: name of seminar, date, location, time (start and finish), topic, speaker's name, objectives, and agenda. Always ask people to RSVP and include your telephone and fax numbers and the contact name.

Finally, to give a sense of urgency to the invitation, add the words "seating is limited."

6. Business directories

If you want to do your own mailing but don't have enough names in your database, make use of directories to build your list of names. Most municipal or regional economic development offices publish and sell directories of local businesses. Many associations publish membership directories while trade show directories can help you find marketing partners.

You can purchase directories from the publisher. Check the yellow pages (another good directory) for the names of directory publishers and expect to pay between $100 and $500. Make sure the publication date of the directory you are interested in is current. If you choose not to purchase the directories, you can access them through government offices and association or public libraries.

5
SHARING THE RISKS:
SPONSORSHIPS AND PARTNERSHIPS

Today's business language is filled with words like strategic alliance, relationship marketing, partnering, and joint venture. These words are more than passing fancies. They represent a trend toward the sharing of risks and rewards among companies with similar goals.

Planning and executing a successful seminar requires a commitment of time, energy, and money. However, you may be able to spread some of the risk and share some benefits by working with marketing partners. The people who are most successful in negotiating sponsorships share a belief in building long-term relationships with the companies they approach. While sponsorship opportunities are most common in the sports and entertainment industries, they are now expanding in the areas of social causes, arts, culture, health, and education.

Cooperative marketing is a tried-and-true technique. You have the ability of widening your exposure in the marketplace by recruiting other companies or associations who stand to benefit from their involvement as partners. If you approach them properly, these marketing partners can be a real boon to your seminar. They can help publicize the event, assist with the logistics, and share the financial burden.

Sound too good to be true? Gaining sponsorship can be a reality if you handle the situation properly. But a word of caution: With cuts in government spending and shrinking company budgets, there is a lot of competition for sponsors, so corporations are inundated with proposals. The secret to having them choose yours is to spark their interest quickly so they give your proposal serious consideration.

a. "WHAT'S IN IT FOR ME?"

Today, everyone with a good idea is looking for sponsorship. Knowing you face a lot of competition, you may ask, "why bother?"

The answer is simple. A sponsor can bring three elements that could spell the difference between success and failure of your seminar. These elements are financial resources, credibility, and exposure. Understanding the impact each of these has on your plans should prove that the effort is worthwhile.

1. Financial resources

Sponsors can help defray the cost of the seminar with a financial contribution or by offering services in kind (i.e., providing its own products or services in lieu of money).

The benefits of a cash contribution are obvious — you have funds that can be allocated to any part of the seminar budget. Services in kind are more specific and may sometimes be limiting.

To get a financial contribution, you need to approach individuals or organizations that will benefit directly from being involved in your seminar but lack the time or services to contribute in lieu of cash. These are companies that are willing to pay for the privilege of being involved. For example, insurance companies or mutual fund managers may be likely prospects if you are offering a financial services seminar. Your own bank manager may be looking to increase his or her small-business portfolio. A retailer may be looking to promote a sale, or a car rental company may want to increase its exposure.

Look to your suppliers for contributions in kind. Your printer may supply a specified number of brochures, a mailing house may provide the cost of a mailing, a local caterer may provide refreshments, and an audiovisual company may set up the seminar room.

2. Credibility

If you are a new player in the community, look for a sponsor with a well-established reputation. By joining marketing forces, you have an opportunity to piggyback on its reputation. The perception is that if a credible company has chosen to sponsor you, you must also be credible.

Radio stations looking to expand their audience may be interested in sponsoring your seminar. Chris McDowall, marketing director at CHFI in Toronto, says the primary reason for his station to consider sponsorship is that the topic will be of interest to the station's listeners. Second, the station is looking for exposure, so visual recognition at the event through banners or other signage will be expected.

Other types of companies that can add credibility to your seminar include telecommunication companies, printers, office supply outfitters, and couriers, all of which are constantly looking for ways to broaden their exposure.

3. Exposure

You can gain exposure by cross-promoting with your partner's marketing efforts. Major marketers do this often. Fast food chains cross-promote all the time through their cash register slips, place mats, and special prizes under bottle caps and on coffee cups. Some major retailers print books of discount coupons which they distribute at the checkout counter. Perhaps they will consider promoting your seminar in such books in exchange for exposure at your seminar.

Find a tie-in and approach a retailer who is interested in your audience. Keep your eyes open. By being creative, you can find partners readily. Many may even have programs in place that you can capitalize on.

Your local chamber of commerce or other service clubs may distribute flyers in the hopes of finding additional members among your seminar guests.

b. WHAT SPONSORS LOOK FOR

Sponsorship is a unique alternative to traditional advertising. Before you approach potential sponsors, research their marketing objectives and tailor your presentation to meet these needs. According to David Disher, manager of Meeting, Convention and Incentive Sales Development at Canadian Airlines International, you should present your potential sponsor with an opportunity to achieve several of their marketing goals. A sponsor will look for two or three doors that their sponsorship can open. They will also look at the potential for recognition beyond the event. Companies are no longer looking for exposure just so they can be good corporate citizens. They are looking for concrete returns. You need to offer them more than their names on a program.

1. Give them what they want

Although exposure may be the pivotal element, it is still only one factor in sponsorship. Companies will be interested in the potential return their sponsorship investments will bring in hard dollars. Many corporations have a model of what the sponsorship contribution should bring to the company. For example, they may look at potential long-term revenue and offer a percentage of this revenue as their contribution.

Sponsors may also be looking for business opportunities — to attract new business or retain existing clients, introduce new products, or launch new promotions. Your target market may offer a prospective sponsor the opportunity to have its name in front of a new audience. The publicity and media attention that your seminar will draw can be very attractive to a sponsor looking to increase its visibility.

Your seminar may give your sponsor an additional way to link its name with the educational component of your seminar. Banks often sponsor business seminars to project the image of being an organization that cares about its clients. Make sure your presentation reflects their needs.

Sponsors may also be interested in your seminar if it fits into their strategic plans. They will be looking for a dramatic link. If there is no fit, they will look elsewhere. Your job is to identify the fit. In short, show them what is in it for them. After that, you have a basis on which to begin negotiations.

You want to be able to show your prospective sponsors both tangible and intangible benefits. The tangibles are measurable benefits that can be seen, heard, or felt. Some of these include publishing the sponsor's name in your advertising and press releases or using its product in sampling. You may offer the sponsor free VIP tickets to your seminar and then rope off an area in the seminar room with a sign that says "Reserved for clients of ABC Corporation."

The intangibles are important as well but harder to quantify. Intangibles involve perception, such as the prestige of being associated with your event. If your topic is stress management, a local spa or health club is a natural sponsor and gives that sponsor an opportunity to reposition and reinforce its products or services. If your seminar is concerned with matters of health or wellness, pharmaceutical companies may be interested. Similarly, plastics companies may want to have their names connected with a seminar on environmental issues.

2. The perfect sponsor

To create a win-win situation, you need to show your prospective sponsors that you understand their objectives and are knowledgeable about their businesses. You must do your homework so that your presentation reflects a genuine interest in each company and does not look as if you are just wanting to grab money. People give money to people, not to organizations, so create the personal rapport that indicates you are sincere.

Understanding the benefits of sponsorship that will accrue to your potential sponsors is the first step in putting your proposal together. But before you start looking for a suitable partner, you need to clarify exactly what you want in a sponsor.

So, who is the perfect sponsor? Your perfect sponsor is a company or organization that has focused on your target market, lots of disposable marketing dollars, a willingness to allocate enough human resources to your project, a strong commitment to your marketing seminar, and the confidence to let you run the show without interference. If this is too good to be true — it is. Finding the perfect sponsor is very difficult.

To facilitate your search, you must be willing to accept compromises along the way. Before starting negotiations, you need to determine exactly what you want. Sponsorship help falls into three broad categories: time, promotion, and money:

(a) *Time.* Making a commitment to do something is one thing, having your sponsor allocate enough time to accomplish it is another.

(b) *Promotion.* For many, spreading the word is the greatest challenge. Find out what distribution channels your sponsor can make available to you and the schedule for each of these.

(c) *Money.* For the most part, your seminar by itself is not going to earn money. Rather, it is a marketing opportunity that will help you expand your business. Your sponsor's financial contribution will help defray operating costs.

Once you have determined how much time, promotion, and money you want from your sponsor, you need to ask, "What am I willing to accept?" Your response will again be a combination of time, promotion, and money. When approaching various potential sponsors, you will quickly learn that they all have their own methods of doing business. Here is where your negotiating skills and willingness to compromise will help you find a suitable compromise between what the sponsor will offer and what you will accept.

3. Beware of the pitfalls

There is no shortage of potential seminar sponsors out there. It is all a matter of finding the right match at the right time. And while the thought of having sponsors is appealing, there are pitfalls.

A friend of mine was busy negotiating a sponsorship agreement only to find out that the company was downsizing and was already stretched to the limit. As a result, although my friend still received a direct benefit, there was a shortage of resources to help her achieve all her goals. She still wanted the relationship with the potential sponsor and decided that the extra work on her part to cover the shortage of resources was worth the effort. Over the past several years, she has continued to work with this sponsor, nurturing its support. Now that the sponsor's situation has turned around, she has benefited from her efforts.

In another instance, a client of mine was involved with a sponsor that had advertising dollars but could not spare the human resources. Once my client understood the problem, the sponsorship arrangement worked out well. He came up with a plan to cover the labor needs and spent the sponsorship money without putting additional stress on the sponsor's staff.

Tom Johnson of the Tom Johnson Marketing Group in London, Ontario, talks about other pitfalls you should be aware of. Beware of the sponsor who wants too much control. Never lose sight of the fact that it is your seminar. Review your objectives and don't sacrifice your own goals to meet the needs of a sponsor.

A sponsor may want to use its own name in the name of your seminar. Before changing the name of your seminar, consider the implications that a potential sponsor's name may have on the attendees. Is this a company who will bring a positive response or one that may be controversial? Do you think that the sponsor's overwhelming presence may cut into other business?

Or a sponsor may want to dictate the site of the seminar because it has an ongoing relationship with a certain hotel chain. While you may be able to get the space free, if it is not accessible to your target audience, it will hurt your seminar.

A seminar planner I know was caught short when a major corporation that was sponsoring a series of her seminars was acquired by a foreign company. The new management had no understanding of her seminars and no desire to be associated with programs connected to the previous owner. It dropped its sponsorship.

A change of personnel within the sponsoring company can lead to problems, too. One of my colleagues researched carefully before meeting with the sponsorship director of a large telecommunications company. She presented her proposal and was delighted with the director's response. Believing in the concept, the director supported the event and laid out an elaborate plan to distribute invitations. My colleague felt everything was in place. However, four weeks before the event, when the invitations were due to be distributed, the director who supported the event was no longer in charge. His replacement was not interested in continuing with the project. My colleague had to scramble madly to get the invitations out on time without the sponsor's help.

Directors of sponsorship come and go regularly. If you are ever caught in a difficult situation regarding a sponsorship contract, bear in mind that the same person may someday be sitting across a desk at another company you may approach later. Take the time to develop a good working relationship with decisionmakers so that when you encounter an obstacle, you can be flexible and look for positive ways to turn the situation around.

c. FINDING AND ATTRACTING SPONSORS

There are numerous ways to find sponsors, and you will have plenty of opportunities if you don't leave your search until the last minute. Typically, corporations need 6 to 12 months to fit sponsorship proposals into their budgets. Find out when your potential sponsor looks at new proposals and how long it takes the company to make a decision.

You will also save a great deal of time if you can talk to the right person first. Decisionmakers can be found in all departments, but sponsorship decisions are usually the responsibility of the marketing, public affairs, or sales department. Start at the top, and ask the right questions to narrow your search.

Concentrate your search on the market you are targeting. If your seminar is aimed at a specific geographic area, there is no point approaching a company that has a national rather than regional marketing plan. You can learn a lot about a company's focus by reading annual reports and news releases in local or business papers and by listening to speeches by top executives.

Use the following list as a guideline for finding sponsors, but don't let it limit your creativity. There are no hard-and-fast rules about the right way to attract sponsors, but you must be proactive, since the chances of a sponsor approaching you are slim.

(a) *Newspapers and magazines.* Look for corporations whose interests are relevant to the subject of your seminar. Read magazines and local newspapers, and pay attention to advertisements to see emerging corporate themes. When you notice who is sponsoring whom in the business and arts section, you will see countless opportunities to tie your seminar to another activity that a corporation or association has adopted. Read corporate announcements. Often when senior executives change companies or positions, they bring their pet causes and interests with them.

(b) *Networking events.* Sponsorship opportunities can be found by networking at business clubs; chambers of commerce; Rotary, Lions, and Kiwanis charity events; and industry meetings. Get involved in a committee and let people know what sponsorship opportunities you are seeking.

(c) *Your vendors.* Your vendors may welcome an opportunity to improve sales of their own products and services by helping you with a marketing seminar. They will likely be interested in the demographic profile of the participants. They may provide money, speakers, promotion, or help with the logistics. It all depends on their perception of your seminar's value to their own business.

(d) *Sponsor competitors.* Approach companies whose competitors are already sponsoring similar seminars. Be prepared to show them how their competition is already benefiting from sponsorship and how their involvement in your seminar will work for them. You should be able to tell them how your seminar differs from the competition's.

(e) *Emerging companies.* Many people immediately gravitate to approaching large organizations as potential sponsors because these companies are either actively involved in sponsorships or they have announced a change in corporate direction. However, there are also many opportunities to get involved with smaller, growing organizations. Although these companies may not bring you the same financial clout or market recognition as the larger ones, their drive, energy, and enthusiasm can make your seminar a success.

(f) *Advertise.* Some newspapers and trade magazines often have a section listing sponsorship opportunities. If there is not such a listing in your local newspaper or trade magazine, you can attract sponsors by placing your own advertisement to capture the attention of prospective sponsors.

d. YOUR PROPOSAL

After identifying a prospective sponsor, your next step is to develop a formal presentation. The presentation may be read by only one person or it may be read by a selection committee. In either case, the merits of your proposal are compared against those of others the company receives. Set measurable objectives and establish realistic expectations that you can give to your potential sponsor.

Your written proposal is often your only opportunity to present your case to a decisionmaker. According to David Disher of Canadian Airlines International, your proposal is like a résumé. The person reading it gets a fix on you and your proposal right away.

Take the time to develop a first-rate presentation that provides the sponsor with a real feel for your seminar and what it's all about. Chris McDowall of CHFI radio asks his potential sponsors to put together a wish list of the type of exposure they are seeking as a basis for discussion.

Your proposal should include the purpose of the seminar, the history of the seminar, the audience, the features, the benefits of attending, your expertise, and the sponsor's investment.

1. Purpose of the seminar

State the purpose of your seminar in words that support your sponsor's values. Saying that you are organizing a seminar to get more leads will likely have little impact on your sponsor. Saying that you are bringing a group of people together to learn something that will improve their businesses or personal lives gives your purpose greater depth.

Your statement of purpose must also ensure that the sponsor's needs will be met. The sponsor wants to know if there will be a fit. Tell the sponsor clearly how your seminar complements its products or services. Tie it into its strategic marketing plan, and show it how this seminar will provide tangible benefits to its customers.

It is also important to show the sponsor that the seminar fits into the company's corporate values, be it education, family, or community. Finally, your statement should include the number of participants you expect to attend the seminar.

Here's an example of a good statement of purpose:

> The purpose of our seminar is to bring together 35, 50- to 60-year-old couples to learn from a nationally recognized expert alternative methods of dealing with their general level of fitness and well-being, as well as learning motivational techniques for improving their overall health.

2. History of the event

If you have run similar seminars in the past, here is a chance to talk about the success of those events. If it is your first seminar, find other businesses that have done something similar to what you plan to do, and outline their results.

3. The audience

Your audience is not one homogeneous mass of people. Each market segment has its own specific traits. Here is the place where you need to define them. (Review chapter 4 on defining your audience.) The more clearly you can define your audience, the easier it will be for a sponsor to make a decision. Define your audience in terms of demographics and psychographics, for example:

> Our target audience is 50- to 60-year-old married couples with an average household income of $100,000. They spend three weeks of each year traveling out of the country, live in the north end of the city, have 3 to 5 grandchildren, and buy 15 books per year.

4. The features

To make the proposal as attractive as possible, develop a list of features. With a little brainstorming, you can come up with a useful list. Some of the features that sponsorship will bring to the sponsor might include:

- Name on signage or banners
- Logo on invitations, brochures, and print ads
- Name on all promotional materials
- Display space
- Use of products in sampling
- Sales opportunities
- Networking opportunities
- Mailing lists of attendees
- Postseminar reports

- Verbal acknowledgment at the seminar
- Invitations for clients and selected guests
- Opportunity to send representatives to the seminar
- Opportunity to introduce the speaker

5. The benefits

Make a list of the benefits that will encourage your potential sponsor to participate. Earlier in this chapter, you learned of the benefits to sponsors. Simply listing all the benefits is a shotgun approach. However, if you do some research in advance, you can tailor your list of benefits to meet the exact needs of your potential sponsor.

6. Your expertise

Before a sponsor puts its name to a project, it must have confidence in the people running the event. Don't be afraid to tell the sponsor of your related accomplishments. It's your credibility that will impress the sponsor. This does not mean that you should include a synopsis of your entire work history. Carefully weave the story of your accomplishments, including details and examples that make you qualified to run this seminar. Ensure that the sponsor believes that you are prepared to invest the time and resources to deliver the seminar successfully. If you have had experience working with other sponsors, say so. If this is your first time, be clear about this as well.

7. The sponsor's investment

Discussing the sponsor's investment is where you get down to the bottom line. As discussed earlier in this chapter, sponsorship parameters include time, money, and promotion. Research potential sponsors to find out the parameters of their sponsorships. If your request for assistance falls within these parameters, you will at least have a chance of a fair hearing.

If you feel there is a match, state clearly what you are looking for. When potential sponsors are inundated with requests, the first ones they reject are those that do not fall within their general parameters. Their decision is based on what they are looking for, rather than on the merits of your proposal. Spell out the value of the sponsorship in dollars, promotion, and labor.

e. HOW SPONSORS MEASURE RESULTS

Every company measures its sponsorship investment differently, depending on its marketing goals. It's important to talk to sponsors about their objectives so that you can collect the necessary data to help them measure and evaluate their investment after the seminar.

If you are planning to run a series of seminars, you may want to approach a sponsor more than once. Providing proper reports promptly after the seminar will greatly enhance your chances of signing up that sponsor again.

Your sponsor may measure results either quantitatively, qualitatively, or both. Which method your sponsor chooses will influence the way in which you evaluate the seminar.

1. Quantitative results

Quantitative results are clear, empirical results focusing on those things that can be measured. Determining which things the sponsor wants to measure depends on the sponsor's needs. After consultation with your sponsor, you will be able to develop a plan, which may include measuring some of the following:

- Number of participants
- Number of brochures distributed
- Number of hits from print, radio, television, flyers, signage
- Number of surveys returned

105

- Number of on-site sign-ups

- Number of other sponsors participating

Some sponsors will ask for a measurement of impressions. Impressions measure impact and are the number of times the sponsor's name appears in the media multiplied by the number of people who are apt to read it or hear it.

2. Qualitative results

Qualitative results are subjective and based on information gathered through conversations, interviews, and personal observations. This is gathered by having people on-site talking to attendees or by holding postseminar telephone interviews. Questions to ask include:

- What do you plan to change as a result of tonight's seminar?

- What do you need to help you implement the suggestions you heard tonight?

Compile for your sponsor the answers to these questions immediately after the seminar. From your report, your sponsor will be able to judge the impact of its sponsorship and decide whether or not to do it again.

f. HOW MUCH DO YOU ASK FOR?

Prospecting seminars are not usually offered to sponsors for monetary gain but rather to create an opportunity to expand business for you and your sponsor. Your sponsor's commitment can involve both a direct financial contribution and hidden costs such as the cost of human resources and general administration. Other costs include initiatives the sponsor develops to complement its involvement and support in your program, such as give-away items, couponing, sampling, and additional mailings. Some sponsors spend double or triple their cash contribution in other expenses in order to leverage their participation.

A good approach to take is to rationalize the sponsor's investment on a cost-per-participant basis. Advertising dollars are often allocated on the basis of their reach. If you can show your sponsor that it will cost $X to reach each person and you explain the advantage of doing so, you are likely to be rewarded with a positive reply to your sponsorship proposal.

It is important to know what you are looking for, but you also must be prepared to work closely with your potential sponsor to find what will work for it. You may need to help your sponsor find a way to be involved. One solution is to develop different levels of sponsorship. As a result, you might have multiple sponsors for one seminar. Be sure to make all sponsors aware of each other's involvement. If a sponsor requests exclusivity, that is, it requests that it be the only provider of a certain product or service, you will have to look for sponsors in unrelated, noncompetitive fields.

You might suggest a tiered sponsorship, in which each tier has a different investment and a different package of benefits. The most common form of tiered sponsorship is "gold, silver, and bronze" levels.

You may find it more acceptable to offer your sponsors an opportunity to sponsor specific parts of your seminar, such as the room, refreshments, audiovisual equipment, or speaker's fees. This will appeal to companies marketing particular services that could offer you such services in lieu of money.

g. THE CONTRACT

Once you have reached an agreement with your sponsor, you will want to write a formal agreement. The contract should include these elements:

- Sponsorship description (name of the seminar, date, and type of sponsorship)

- Roles and responsibilities of the sponsor and your company

- Media benefits: what promotions will be involved

- Other benefits

- Exclusivity arrangement

- Length of the agreement

- First right of refusal on sponsorship of next seminar

- Favorable positioning in relation to its competitors

- Length of exposure (is there an opportunity for a series?)

h. FOLLOW-UP

After the seminar is over, immediately send thank-you notes to all your sponsors. Provide them with a report including attendance figures, advertising statistics, copies of editorial and media coverage, copies of press releases, and participant evaluations.

Ask each sponsor for feedback, including its level of satisfaction with its participation. Ask for any further suggestions.

Keep samples of promotional materials that have sponsors' names on them to help you recruit sponsors for future seminars.

Sponsorship can be a real boost to your seminar or an incredible burden. If you choose to ask for help, do so with your eyes open. If you jump in unprepared, you are just asking for trouble. A good sponsorship relationship can result in a successful seminar and pave the way for future marketing seminars.

6
BRING ON THE PROS:
USING A GUEST SPEAKER

You have two choices: you can make the presentation yourself or you can hire a guest speaker. Some people welcome the opportunity to speak at their own events, while for others, the thought of standing in front of a group of strangers is unthinkable.

There are pros and cons to both options. If you decide to make the presentation yourself, you have much more planning to do in terms of delivering your material (see chapter 7). If you choose to have a guest speaker, you still have a public role as master of ceremonies. (Details on performing this role are also included in chapter 7.)

a. TO SPEAK OR NOT TO SPEAK

Your guests are coming to your seminar to learn something new. They may also be attracted by who is delivering this information. This does not mean that you cannot make the presentation yourself, but you should realize that there may be times when it is better to have someone else give the talk.

Presenting the material yourself, if you can do it effectively, is a great way to impress your audience. You are the expert. You create the examples, and you answer all the questions. You follow up with your participants personally, and there is no added expense.

On the other hand, you may decide to use a guest presenter because you feel you lack in-depth knowledge of the field, you want a name closely linked to success in the field, you believe someone else will have greater drawing power, or you are not ready to take on this challenge.

Guest speakers, if well-known, can add a measure of credibility to your seminar. Every business field has people who are well-recognized as experts. These people may be independent speakers who have developed reputations, for example as a well-known chef or gardener. Representatives from your own industry, including senior executives, managers, or technical experts, may also be attractive as speakers.

On the other hand, guest speakers usually don't follow up personally with the seminar participants, they can be costly, and their presentations are often "packaged," rather than developed for a specific audience.

Whichever option you choose should be measured against your comfort level, budget, and the availability of an appropriate guest speaker.

1. Your comfort level

When you think of comfort, think about both your ability to make the presentation and your familiarity with the material. Let's look at both.

Making a presentation in front of a group can be a tremendously gratifying experience. For some people it comes easily, while others struggle with feelings of self-doubt. During your seminar, you will have to say a few introductory words to the audience. Making the whole presentation can be nothing more than a continuation of these introductory remarks. Most inexperienced speakers find that their comfort level grows once they begin to speak. As they develop rapport with their audience, they relax.

However, the first step involves your willingness to speak in front of a group of strangers. For those of you who decide to take up the challenge, the next chapter offers a detailed analysis of your presentation, tips on how to overcome your fears, how to structure and deliver your presentation, and the effective use of audiovisual equipment.

If the fear of public speaking is so great that you would rather die first than stand in front of an audience, hiring a guest speaker will solve your problems.

Many inexperienced presenters consider their ability to handle the material as the most important consideration. But, making a good presentation means more than having a good set of overheads. It also depends on how well you handle questions and explain complicated material so it is clear and meaningful to your audience. You may be relatively new to your industry and unfamiliar with recent regulatory changes or new products. This should not stop you. There is an old saying that "the best way to learn is to teach."

By studying the material and presenting it so it addresses your audience's concerns, you will be able to get your message across.

2. Budget

A well-known speaker may command a fee which could drain your budget. Your challenge then is to find guest speakers you can afford. Here's where networking helps. One place to look is with your suppliers. They may be willing to send one of their own representatives to speak at your event. An import/export consultant I know ran a successful seminar by asking the freight forwarder he worked with to make the presentation. The freight forwarder was looking to expand his own business and welcomed the opportunity to speak in front of potential clients at no charge.

Some industries will provide speakers to independent distributors for their prospecting seminars. In the health care industry, where educating the public about products is essential to success, doctors are often asked to conduct seminars. In Ontario, a pharmaceutical company retained a gynecologist to conduct a road show on the pros and cons of

hormone replacement therapy. The financial services industry often retains best-selling authors in the field of investment, retirement savings, or home buying. Travel agencies
touting a new cruise line might have the captain and some
crew members attend a slide presentation and speak to the
audience about the ship's amenities.

A sponsor will sometimes pay the speaker's fees if the
topic relates to its business. Or it may send one of its people
to make the presentation. A garden center ran a seminar
sponsored by a seed company, so the sponsor sent a horticul-
turist to give a talk. The sponsor may also cover some of the
speaker's expenses, such as hotel room, car rental, and air-
fare.

Finding creative ways to help offset the cost of the
speaker can save you money, but you should be aware of
potential strings attached. For example, your sponsor may
want to influence the direction of your seminar. This might
not be a bad thing if you feel that your guests are still getting
good value and you can still meet your objectives. However,
if the sponsor is looking for an advertisement, this could have
a negative impact on your seminar. It is *your* program, so *your*
credibility is on the line. Your first objective is to ensure that
your guests get something of value for their time. All fluff
and little substance are not what your audience is looking for.

If you need sponsorship help with the guest speaker, do
your homework carefully. Meet with or telephone the potential sponsor to ensure your goals are compatible.

3. The right speaker

Some speakers will be more suitable for your seminar than
others. Some speakers have significant drawing power and
will attract a large audience. However, be sure your guest
will attract the right audience — people who are also interested in your products or services. A room full of people who
are there simply to hear a celebrity speak may not represent

your target market. You need to link your speaker with your objectives. Don't hire just a name.

b. WHERE TO FIND GUEST SPEAKERS

There are many sources of qualified speakers. Referrals from colleagues who have heard good speakers or use speakers they are happy with are the most reliable source. Use your network and listen to other people's experiences with speakers.

Consider the following:

- Universities and colleges have lists of professors who are willing to speak.

- Government offices have consultants who are experts in their fields.

- Professional associations, chambers of commerce, and boards of trade can recommend members who speak on various topics.

- Speakers' bureaus, though sometimes expensive, should also be considered. State your budget up-front.

You can also find people who will speak for free. With corporate downsizing, many professionals are moving into the world of entrepreneurship. Others looking to change their careers or searching for new clients may consider your audience the right target.

Entertainers may be interested in testing out new material. Authors look for exposure when they are launching a new book. However, a word of caution on this last one: Just because someone has written a book and is considered an expert in his or her field does not mean he or she is a good speaker. Authors write. Speakers speak. Although many authors are good speakers, you want to be sure the one you approach is — before your seminar. Don't be dazzled by big names: ask for referrals.

c. HIRING A GUEST SPEAKER

Before you finalize your arrangements with a speaker, it is a good idea to hear him or her speak at a public venue. If this is not possible, ask for referrals from clients who have used the speaker. When you call these referrals, ask questions that relate to the desired outcome of your seminar.

Here are some questions you might want to ask:

(a) Was the speaker willing to customize the presentation for your audience?

(b) Did the speaker spend time (either on the telephone or in person) learning more about your seminar and its objective?

(c) Did the speaker stick to the topic?

(d) Did the speaker deliver what you wanted?

(e) Was the speaker's style formal or informal?

(f) Was the speaker willing to answer your audience's questions?

(g) Was the speaker willing to stay after the presentation to answer one-on-one questions?

(h) How did your audience respond to the speaker?

(i) Did the speaker take too much time pitching his or her books and tapes?

(j) Would you hire this speaker again?

Once you do decide on a speaker, make sure you sign a written contract spelling out each of your roles and responsibilities. This can be as simple as a letter outlining the terms of agreement. If you use a speaker's bureau, the bureau will prepare a contract. Many professional speakers have their own contracts which they will ask you to sign.

Your contract should include:

(a) *Financial clauses.* Include the terms of payment, when a deposit is due, which expenses are covered by you and which by the speaker, and whether receipts are required. Allowable expenses should be carefully determined and itemized in the contract. By leaving expenses to the discretion of your speaker, you may face some additional costs that you hadn't considered, such as business-class travel or upgraded hotel rooms. Include responsibility for often-overlooked costs such as preparation time, couriers, and telephone calls.

(b) *Expectations.* Spell out your expectations for the speaker. These include expected time of arrival, starting time of event, length of presentation, length of time you expect the speaker to stay at the seminar, whether he or she will network with the guests and handle the question-and-answer period, and whether he or she will participate in a panel discussion.

(c) *Handout material.* Specify whether the speaker is to bring copies for everyone or provide an original for duplication.

(d) *Cancellation policy.* Specify whether the speaker gets paid if you cancel. Agree on a deadline for cancellation without a fee and discuss what happens to the deposit if the speaker has to cancel.

(e) *Logistics.* What audiovisual equipment does the speaker require? Does the speaker have a preferred seating arrangement? May you tape the presentation? Will you allow the speaker to sell his or her own materials at the end of the event? Determine this and write it into the contract.

(f) *Evaluation.* Specify in writing that you plan to have your participants evaluate the presentation. Often experienced guest speakers can provide helpful suggestions for preparing the evaluation form.

d. PREPARING YOUR GUEST SPEAKER

Once an agreement has been reached, spend some time talking to the speaker. State your seminar objectives to ensure that his or her content is compatible with your goals. You should define as clearly as possible your target audience to ensure the speech is relevant and in a language your audience will relate to. If your audience is new to the topic, ask your speaker to avoid jargon. Ask the speaker to build references to your business into the presentation. They can be as simple as, "I am sure that your host, Bill, is willing to meet with you later to discuss your personal needs."

If you haven't seen your speaker in action, be sure to discuss speaking style. You need to know if he or she is comfortable speaking in the environment you have created for your seminar, be it formal or informal.

Will your speaker speak from a podium or work the room with a portable microphone? Is he or she comfortable with spontaneous questions from the floor? Your goal is to make your audience as comfortable as possible. Matching your speaker's style to your audience is key to achieving this goal.

e. HAVE A BACKUP

Murphy's Law is proven true particularly when you are relying on other people. When using a guest speaker, there are all sorts of contingencies you must allow for: weather, health of the speaker, flight schedules, traffic, power failures, and getting lost, to name a few. What do you do when everyone shows except the guest speaker?

There are many things you can do to ensure the safe arrival of your speaker. If he or she is from out of town, have a copy of his or her travel and accommodation schedule. On the day of the seminar, confirm the schedule with the carriers.

Plan to contact the speaker early in the day to make sure everything is on schedule. It is also helpful to have an emergency telephone number, just in case you want to get in touch with the speaker at the last minute. And be sure to give the speaker a telephone number where he or she can reach you, if necessary.

With every detail taken care of, something can still happen at the last minute. *Always have a backup plan.* You might consider:

- checking with your local library or video rental store on the availability of a suitable video that can help you through the presentation,

- having another speaker ready "just in case," or

- giving the presentation yourself.

7

POWERFUL PRESENTATIONS

If you have decided to make the presentation yourself, consider this chapter your personal coach. There are many excellent books and courses that will explain the nuts and bolts of making a presentation. Some of these are listed in Appendix 2. My intent in this chapter is to familiarize you with what's involved in making successful presentations. We will examine all the elements of a good presentation: planning, delivery skills, the use of audiovisual tools, tips to control nervousness, and effective handling of questions, as well as techniques that veteran presenters use to handle their audience.

a. THREE PLANNING STEPS

1. The presentation objective

The first step in any activity is to state your objective: What do you want from your presentation? The answer to that question may be different from your seminar objective that you defined in chapter 2.

Your presentation objective is a statement that clearly defines what you and your audience will get out of the presentation. It is a projection into the future. It boils down to completing this simple statement: "After the presentation, my audience will _____." Some possible answers are —

- Want to meet with a consultant to discuss this in more detail

- Join an organization dedicated to this cause

- Become involved in the business

- Buy a product or use a service

- Make a lifestyle change

However you completed the sentence, state it up front as your first step toward a focused presentation.

The next part of the objective is to ensure that your audience will always get something out of your presentation. Unless there is a benefit for your audience, the chances of motivating it to action is slim. Examples of benefits to participants include:

- Increasing their general state of health and giving them more energy

- Providing them with a worry-free retirement

- Making them feel more positive about their environment

- Helping them save money

Your statement of objectives can be summarized into this short sentence: "After the presentation, my audience will _____ because it means _____ to them."

2. Understand your audience

In chapter 4, you read how important it was to analyze your target audience. You learned to identify your audience in both demographic and psychographic terms. Armed with that basic understanding, you are now prepared to go one step further. You want to explore their willingness to accept the information you have to present, and to do that, you should consider three points: outlook, level of knowledge, and attitude.

(a) Outlook

What influences the outlook of the people in your audience? Parents might focus on how financial planning affects their children; doctors will want to know the scientific reasons for choosing one product over another; engineers might want detailed descriptions about how a product works; artists might want to see the big picture and ignore the details.

No single outlook is better than another. It is all a matter of understanding your audience's needs and choosing the best way of communicating meaningful information.

(b) Level of knowledge

Often, speakers are in a quandary about how to address their audience. You should know your audience's level of understanding before deciding how to position your information. Should you speak to the audience as if all members are knowledgeable about the topic, and risk talking over the heads of those who know very little? Or should you focus on those with little understanding of your topic and risk boring those who know a lot?

The answer is to focus on your audience and its needs. This is best accomplished by determining how much participants already understand. Some seminars have participants from all levels in one room. In this case, you would aim toward the middle level. Try to determine participants' level of knowledge when they are preregistering, or by asking a few short questions at the beginning of your presentation if you are able to adjust your presentation on the spot

(c) Attitude

Understanding how your audience feels about a certain topic will also be very helpful. On close examination, you may find ambivalence or, alternatively, very strong feelings about what you are presenting. Understanding some of these attitudes can help you adjust your presentation to your audience. Try to learn about participants' attitudes by asking as they register, "How do you feel about this topic?" This questions can reveal some interesting answers.

3. The content

Often, presenters collect all the relevant information and then decide what to include and what to leave out. However, it is much more efficient if you find out what the audience needs to know *before* you start gathering information.

If you have developed a clear idea of what you want; what the benefits of your seminar are to your audience; and what your audience's outlook, level of knowledge, and attitude are, you are ready to develop the presentation outline.

Before you run to the library and sift through the piles of books, take a moment and reflect on the work you have already done. Ask yourself this question: "What information is most important to my audience so that I can achieve my objectives and participants will see a benefit?"

For example, assume that you are selling a financial service and the purpose of your seminar is to recruit new clients. If your audience is composed of highly sophisticated investors, your analysis will look like this:

> *Outlook:* a lot of experience and much financial savvy.
> *Level of knowledge:* significant.
> *Attitude:* interested but skeptical.
> *Content:* details of a new financial approach; track record of the financial institution behind this concept; comparisons between this new approach and some traditional ones.

With this information in hand, you can begin work on your content. In this example, you will have to provide some forceful arguments to be persuasive. Ask yourself this second question: "What compelling arguments will overcome their doubts?" Not everyone will be skeptical, but if you assume that they will be, you are better prepared to give a more persuasive argument. If you can convince the skeptic, you can convince anyone.

These compelling arguments come in proof statements. Proof statements take a variety of forms, including case studies, financial projections, annual reports, and testimonials. By knowing your audience, you can pick the proof statement that wins it over. You will need a few proofs for each content item.

Once you have thought about how you will make your argument, you are ready to begin researching the information you need, focusing on your audience's need.

Remember to plan the overall timing of your presentation. One of the challenges most speakers face is delivering the right amount of information. It all boils down to simple arithmetic. If your presentation is one hour and if you leave 5 minutes for an introduction and 5 minutes to close, you have 50 minutes for the main body of the presentation. If you have three points of equal importance, that leaves approximately 17 minutes for each.

As you are researching, keep this number in mind. If you have too much information for that length of time, keep your audience's needs in mind and ask yourself, "What information is most compelling?" Faced with a short amount of time, you want to throw out the fluff and stick to the meat and potatoes.

b. PULLING IT ALL TOGETHER

1. Presentation formulas

Your goal is to keep your presentation entertaining as well as educational. The content should include practical how-to information delivered concisely. Try to talk from your own experience. This technique raises your credibility and helps develop rapport with your audience.

You also want to keep the presentation simple. Provide a few central points to whet the audience's appetite. You want participants to call on you after the seminar. Research shows that people can remember a maximum of five points, so limit your presentation to three to five main points.

Seminar participants will enjoy the seminar more if they are actively involved in it. Try some of the techniques used by successful trainers, such as role playing, brainstorming, and small group discussions.

For maximum impact, organize your material using the old newspaper formula: tell them what you're going to tell them, tell them, and then tell them what you've just told them. This formula follows the three crucial parts of a good presentation: the opening, the body, and the close. Each step is important to keep you and your audience on the same track.

When following this formula, you will be aware of the repetition. Don't worry; it's necessary. There is a lot of detail your audience must absorb and you cannot assume that everyone in the audience will follow everything you say. Repetition helps reinforce significant points and ensures that your audience is following along. It is also a great way to bridge the gap that sometimes occurs in an audience where there are different levels of knowledge and experience.

2. The opening: tell them what you are going to tell them

(a) State the purpose

The purpose of the opening is to begin a journey with your audience. When you last took an airplane flight, you were introduced to the crew via the intercom before the journey began. The flight attendant welcomed you and told you all the safety rules, then the captain let you know about the flight plan and other interesting information. By doing this, the crew ensured that all the passengers were on the right plane, going in the same direction.

Your opening has the same purpose as the introduction on the airplane. You need to give the purpose of the talk, establish rapport, establish credibility, explain the logistics, and give the audience a road map of what will follow.

The purpose of the presentation relates to the audience's interest and needs. The purpose was stated in your promotional material. By restating the purpose at the start of your presentation, you are once again ensuring that you are all on the same flight plan and that there has been no misunderstanding.

I remember hearing a politician speak to a ratepayers group. He had left his office for the meeting in a hurry and took with him the wrong speech. He began without stating the purpose of the presentation, instead jumping directly into the body. The audience was bewildered. It had no idea what he was talking about and where he was going. It took the audience (and presumably the politician) quite a few minutes to realize the mistake. If he had stated his purpose up front, the mistake would have been caught sooner.

Here are some example of purpose statements:

> "The purpose of this presentation is to give you some up-to-date financial information that will be crucial to you when making your retirement decisions."

or

> "Our objective tonight is to introduce you to some new products that are sure to have a positive impact on your approach to holistic medicine."

or

> "Tonight, I want to acquaint you with a vacation alternative that will change the way you plan your annual holidays."

(b) Establish rapport

Next, you want to establish rapport. You started to build rapport when you greeted each guest at the door; now you want to make sure that the audience as a whole is comfortable not only with you but also with each other. A few words from you will accomplish this.

Barreling into your presentation without establishing rapport gets your presentation off to an awkward beginning that does nothing to put the audience at ease. Begin by welcoming your audience. A simple statement such as, "I'd like to welcome you all here tonight" or "I know the traffic was heavy and I really appreciate you all being here" will suffice.

You might also build rapport by relating a personal story and some background information about yourself. You might say, "When I first learned about this product, I was in a seminar such as this and was wondering what I was doing there. Well, I assure you that I became one of the converted. I am really excited about the possibilities and look forward to sharing this information with you today."

To help your audience develop rapport with each other, you might start with a short icebreaker. If it's a small group, ask everyone to introduce themselves one by one to the others, reveal a bit about their background, and state their objectives for attending the seminar. For larger groups, you may consider having the group stand up and hand out business cards or introduce themselves to their neighbors. If you choose to do this, it is important to put a time limit on the activity. For example, you could say, "In the next two minutes, please

125

introduce yourself to the people on each side of you and then turn around and meet the person behind you."

Another technique is to ask the audience questions and ask for a show of hands. Questions should set the mood and introduce the topic. Instead of asking, "How many of you had a difficult time getting here tonight?" ask "How many of you have read about this topic?" or "Have you heard someone speak on this topic before?"

Several books on icebreakers are available. One that I particularly like is *Games Trainers Play* by Ed Scannell, published by Prentice Hall.

(c) Establish credibility

Your credibility is crucial to your audience's acceptance of the information you are about to give. If you ignore this step, you open yourself up to criticism and skepticism. Although you may not be a polished speaker, your credibility is in your product knowledge, your understanding of your community, or your experience as a user of the products or services. Your statement of credibility might sound like this:

"I first started investing for my retirement 15 years ago — long before I ever thought about getting into this industry. During those years, I asked a lot of questions and learned a great deal. I would like to pass some of it along to you tonight."

(d) Explain the logistics

Part of your responsibility is to make sure your guests are comfortable in their surroundings. This happens when they understand what will be happening at the seminar. A quick explanation of the logistics of the event is appropriate.

When you think of logistics, think about those things that your audience is going to want to know about. Some of these things you will have taken care of when you greeted people at the door, others will need to be attended to now. These logistics include when the seminar will finish, when breaks will occur, washroom locations, details of refreshments, and the question-and-answer format your seminar will take.

(e) Give the audience a road map

Here is your chance to map out the direction of the presentation. Tell your guests what you are going to tell them. Present a list of the main points your presentation will cover, and tell them how each point will be of benefit to them.

You may wish to list the agenda on a flip chart or use an overhead transparency. Having a visual list as reference helps your audience keep up with you.

Here are some examples of verbal road maps:

"During the next hour, I will show you the details of a new financial approach and how it may fit into your planning. I will outline the track record of the financial institution behind this concept so you will feel comfortable with the principles. And I will provide you with a comparison between this new approach and some traditional approaches so that you can compare their features and benefits."

or

"During this presentation, you will hear how continued use of our herbal supplement will increase your energy level and not affect the soundness of your sleep. You will also see how the continued use of these supplements will add to your youthful appearance and how these products will help you in the ongoing battle of weight control. We will examine some exciting research conducted at MIT that I know you will find compelling."

or

"I will review our new approach to time-
share and compare the traditional approach
so that you can make your decision with
accuracy and confidence. I will also show
how you can convert your existing time-
share into the new plan, as well as present
you with some exciting opportunities that
will give you even more flexibility than you
had before."

(f) Bridge to the presentation

You now move to the body of the presentation by bridging
the opening to the agenda items. Your bridging statement
doesn't need to be complicated. Just use a simple statement
such as, "So, let me get into the details."

3. The body: tell them

The body is the meat of the presentation. This is what your
audience has been waiting for. With a solid opening, your
audience knows what to expect and the order in which each
point will be presented. Your job then is to present the
information in a clear, concise manner. This requires presenting each item, one at a time, followed by the relevant statement of proof.

Each section of the body should be presented like this:

Bridge
Point #1
Proof statements
Bridge
Point #2
Proof statements
Bridge
Point #3
Proof statements

Handle each point separately and check back with your audience to see if it has grasped the point before moving on to the next one. Hold your audience's attention with each new point by mentioning the benefit it can expect from the next point. Say something like, "This next point is really important because it will help you . . ." or "You may want to jot this next point down so you can . . ."

Be aware of your audience's attention span. There is an old adage that the mind can absorb only what the seat of the pants can tolerate. If the audience looks like it needs a break, take one.

4. The close: tell them what you've just told them

Your close is a summary and call for action. It is your opportunity to leave your audience with a challenge to apply what it has learned and take the next step. Don't ad lib your ending. Leave your presentation on a positive note with a good close. You can include a success story which can be a very powerful example and then go through the following closing steps:

(a) summation of the presentation,

(b) call to action, and

(c) final rapport statement.

(a) Summation of the presentation

Tell them what you have just told them. This step helps the audience by putting the whole presentation into a neat mental package. Your summation will crystallize the entire content of the presentation and put it into context for the audience. It is your opportunity to link all the benefits and proofs into one powerful statement that will bring home the importance and urgency of your information. Here are some examples:

> "You have seen how this new approach can dovetail your existing financial plans. It offers you an opportunity to ensure that

your retirement is safe and comfortable, and finally, it gives you the flexibility to take advantage of new opportunities when they arise, which can mean even greater rewards."

or

"You have learned that our products can bring you an increased level of energy and add to your youthful appearance. We have also shown how we can help you maintain the proper weight for your height and age."

or

"You see, time-share is a whole new ball game. It is a new approach that will change the way you look at vacation planning. It is open to everyone, whether you own a time-share now or not, and it gives you more flexibility than you thought possible."

(b) Call to action

If you have built a persuasive case, your call to action will be expected. A call to action is your asking the audience to react in some way to the information it has received. It can be as simple as, "I am looking forward to working with each of you individually to explore natural health remedies" or "I hope you will consider this information and start your own recycling program" or "For more details, please take the information sheets that are on the table home with you."

The call to action is not just for selling situations; it works in any situation. If you want your audience to take some action, ask it to.

(c) Final rapport statement

Your presentation began with a rapport statement, which was your way to relax the audience and get it into a positive mood. During the presentation, you should have done whatever possible to maintain this mood. Now, at the end of the presentation, you have one last opportunity to leave the audience with a positive feeling about you and your information.

A final rapport statement can be "Thank you for agreeing to spend this evening with me exploring this new technology" or "I have really enjoyed having you attend my seminar, and I hope you have a safe drive home."

c. INTRODUCING AND THANKING THE GUEST SPEAKER

If you are planning to use a guest speaker, you still need to hone your presentation skills to ensure the success of your seminar. As master of ceremonies, you will be responsible for introducing and thanking the speaker. You want to use this time to reinforce to your audience that it is *your* seminar; the more visible you are during the event, the stronger the impression you will make.

1. The introduction

Your introduction of the guest speaker is an excellent opportunity for you to create a good mood in the room and set up the seminar. Before you begin to prepare your introduction, ask your guest speaker for a prepared biography. Find out how he or she would like you to handle the introduction. Some speakers want the prepared biography to be read exactly as written, while others provide it as a guideline only.

Ask the speaker how he or she will handle the opening of the talk. You want to make sure your introduction is a natural lead into the speech and there is no redundancy.

A good introduction includes some of the same steps outlined for preparing your opening (see section **b.2.** above). You don't want to steal any of the thunder away from the speaker, but you do want to ensure that everything is covered.

You still want to create rapport, explain the logistics, and establish credibility.

(a) Create rapport

Many of the steps mentioned previously also apply here. Often the guest speaker will want to take on the task of warming up the audience with a quick networking exercise. If so, you will obviously not take on this job. But if the speaker would rather have you handle this part, do so. To create rapport, ensure that you welcome everyone to the seminar and introduce yourself: "I would like to thank you all for being here tonight. We have an interesting program set up for you that I know you will enjoy. My name is Barbara Siskind and I am your host."

(b) Explain the logistics

This step is identical to step three of "The opening," covered earlier in this chapter (see section **b.2.**). Seldom will your guest speaker want to handle this aspect of the presentation, so be prepared.

(c) Establish credibility

Your introduction should tell your audience why this person is qualified and what participants will be learning. Then simply say, "Ladies and gentlemen, I am pleased to introduce Mr. Lee," and hand the microphone over to your guest speaker.

2. The thank-you

Your thank-you is your opportunity to bridge the speaker's comments to your seminar objectives. This is the time to deftly reinforce the important points the speaker made and point out how they fit into your services. You may want to jot down notes during the presentation to help do this. You are thanking the speaker on behalf of the audience, so you will want to echo their thoughts. Reflect on how the information will be of value to your guests.

For example, you might say:

> "Mr. Lee brought out some important information that we are all grateful to learn. Before I became a financial consultant, I had no idea how important financial planning was. Mr. Lee has echoed some of the things I learned early in my career that have helped me not only in my ability to help my clients but to take care of my personal financial planning. I feel better knowing my retirement is secure, and I know you will as well."

or

> "I am reluctant to use this old cliché, but these products really have changed my life. After hearing Mr. Lee's presentation and the compelling MIT research results, I am sure you will agree that it is worth taking a serious look at this age-old medical alternative."

or

> "I remember when I bought my first time-share. In those days, you owned your property for 25 years, then it reverted to the developer. Much has changed since those early days, and the new approach outlined by Mr. Lee is a good example of why time-share is worth a second look."

d. HONING YOUR DELIVERY SKILLS

If you are not an experienced speaker, try watching good speakers, both in person and on television. Observe their body language, how they handle the audience, hold the audience's attention, answer questions, and motivate and stimulate. If you are not confident about your speaking ability, remember that you will improve with practice. Here are some tips to help you become a more successful speaker:

- Use personal information to create rapport with the audience.

- Develop a simple and effective presentation.

- Use presentation notes to keep on track.

- Open with an attention-getter.

- Use quotations and statistics to back up your presentation.

- Use stories as much as possible to make your point.

- Familiarize yourself with the audiovisual equipment.

- Maintain eye contact with the audience.

- Use appropriate nonverbal gestures.

- Speak at a controlled volume.

- Speak with enthusiasm and sincerity.

- Be persuasive but not high pressure.

- Maintain a comfortable stance to avoid appearing nervous.

- Have a forceful close.

- Be respectful of time.

- Use humor with discretion: most jokes offend someone.

A good speaker involves the audience. The audience enjoys the experience, identifies with the speaker, and comes away committed.

Practice your presentation aloud once or twice, but don't overdo it since you don't want to sound rehearsed.

To keep yourself on track, it's a good idea to use presentation notes. Do not write your speech out in longhand. Your presentation notes are a summary of the significant points with the corresponding visuals and the timing of each part. Sample #5 shows a presentation outline; you shouldn't need more notes than ones like those shown in this sample.

e. UNDERSTANDING BODY LANGUAGE

Nonverbal messages have powerful impacts. Research has shown that the actual words spoken account for only 7% of someone's impression of you. The paraverbal messages, the way we say what we say — our tone of voice, inflection, and pace — account for 38% of someone's impression. Our nonverbal messages conveyed by body language — our posture, gestures, the clothes we wear — account for 55% of an impression. In short, it's not so much what you say but how you say it and how you look when you are saying it that creates rapport.

1. Smile

A simple smile can help you connect with your audience which looks to you to set the mood. Smile and the whole world smiles with you, frown and . . . you get the point. A smile is a great way to develop rapport. But be cautious. Smile while you are making positive points, but change your facial expression to be consistent with what you are saying: put on a more serious look when talking about critical points.

2. Eye contact

Direct eye contact with audience members makes them more human in your eyes and therefore easier to talk to. Again, it helps you establish and maintain rapport. Avoid focusing on just one person while ignoring the rest of the audience. Look at everyone, pausing to make eye contact with each individual.

Key Points	Visuals	Time
Opening		
• Rapport-building statement		7:30–7:35
• Icebreaker and logistics		7:35–7:45
• Our objective tonight . . .	Overhead #1	7:45–7:50
Bridge		
• So let me get into the details		
Body		
1.	Overhead #2	7:50–8:00
2.	Flip-chart the points	8:00–8:10
3.	Overhead #3	8:10–8:20
Close		
Key elements/Summary		
• So you have seen how . . .	Overhead #4	8:20–8:25
Benefits/Action steps		
• I'm looking forward to . . .		8:25–8:30
• Thank you for coming		

If you want to avoid a heckler or someone who is trying to monopolize the floor, turn your eyes away from that person.

3. Standing

Some speakers are more comfortable working behind a podium; some work best walking around, getting close to the audience. Experience will let you know what works best for you. If you choose to use a podium, remember that it is a tool, not a crutch. Avoid holding it so tightly your knuckles turn white.

If you choose to walk around, never sit down. Standing always adds energy to your presentation and allows you to project your voice better. You breathe more deeply and project your voice more easily.

Your stance sends out a message. Stooped shoulders make you appear nervous and tense. Good posture makes you appear more approachable. You will more effectively make your point by leaning into the audience.

4. Dress

A large part of people's impression of you comes from how they perceive you physically. As unfair as this sounds, how you look really does matter. When thinking about what to wear, keep the words "appropriate" and "professional" in mind.

Appropriate means dressing in a fashion that fits the venue and audience. Professional reflects who you are, so dress for the role. The safest color is dark blue. It's professional and reinforces your professionalism.

Don't ever dress too casually. A good rule to follow is to focus on your audience and dress one step above what they will likely wear. Once your presentation begins, you can take off your jacket and roll up your sleeves.

5. Grooming

Recall the image of Albert Einstein with his frizzy hair and the image of the mad professor comes immediately to mind. You can see this look on T-shirts and posters in shops across North America. This look may be appropriate for someone who has just discovered the theory of relativity, but your neat appearance will give your prospects enough confidence to want to do business with you.

6. Gestures

Well-chosen body and facial gestures can add a sense of drama to your presentation. Think back to the image of the then Soviet premier Nikita Khrushchev in the 1950s pounding a shoe on the table at the United Nations. Certainly a dramatic gesture.

Your gestures need not be that extreme. The best way to learn new gestures and determine which works best for you is to watch professional speakers. Observe their nonverbal behavior. Watch and learn, then integrate these nonverbal messages into your presentation style.

Don't put your hands in your pockets or leave them locked behind your back, but rather, let your arms move with the natural flow of your body. As you proceed with your presentation, you may want to unbutton your jacket or roll up your sleeves to let your audience know that you are getting down to business.

7. Reading your audience

Finally, don't forget that body language works both ways. You need to project a certain image to your audience, but you also need to be able to pick up on the signals your audience is giving you, expressed through participants' body language.

When you look out into the sea of faces, you see a group of individuals who have all chosen to attend your seminar for their own individual reasons. Some are there to learn, some are there to spy for your competitors, while yet others may have been dragged there unwillingly by a spouse or friend. You cannot be everything to everyone. However, by reading your audience's nonverbal messages, you will be able to do all you can to ensure that participants get as much as possible from the presentation. Are their needs being satisfied? Are you getting through? Is the material relevant? Is the flow of information targeted properly? None of these questions can be answered properly until after the presentation is over and you ask for feedback. But you can glean clues along the way. If you are perceptive, watching your audience's nonverbal behavior can give you valuable pointers to follow.

Ignoring such signals can result in disaster. You may start getting off track and lose parts of the audience, the audience may stop listening, or it may just need to take a break. Responding to the clues will help you deliver a well-balanced, well-accepted presentation.

In his book *How to Develop and Promote Successful Seminars and Workshops* published by John Wiley and Sons, Howard L. Shenson lists 15 nonverbal messages and their possible meanings. The following are some of the common nonverbal messages you may see at your seminar.

- *Folded arms.* Arms folded across the chest sends the message that the person may be closed to your ideas and may need further proof to be convinced.

- *Crossed legs.* Like folded arms, crossed legs may send the message that the person is closed to your ideas and needs to be convinced. Crossing and uncrossing of legs can also be a sign of boredom.

- *Sitting on the edge of the seat.* This person is probably very responsive and interested in your message. Use this person as an ally if you need one.

- *Tilted head.* Tilting the head can show an interest in learning more. As with the person sitting on the edge of the seat, the head-tilter can be an ally.

- *Deep breathing.* Deep breathing often indicates that the person is frustrated with your message or presentation. This person may be giving you the message that he or she would rather be somewhere else.

- *Clenched fists.* This person has probably moved beyond frustration and is getting angry. This might be a clue to call a break.

f. OVERCOMING NERVOUSNESS: PUTTING THE BUTTERFLIES IN ORDER

Trying to eliminate all your nervousness may not be realistic. But you can control it. Most inexperienced speakers often experience nervousness accompanied by a huge dose of self-doubt. For many of us, public speaking is not something we do often enough to get comfortable with. Here are a few tips that will help you round up the butterflies that are roaming through your insides and rechannel that nervousness into positive energy to give you an edge and keep your presentation lively and interesting.

1. Rehearse

A speaker once said that the three most important things you can do to overcome your nervousness are rehearse, rehearse, and rehearse.

Rehearsing gives you confidence in the material and allows you to iron out all the wrinkles. If you know your stuff, there is less chance you will have to read your notes. Once you feel confident, stop and put your prepared text away.

But beware! Over-rehearsing can be as deadly as under-rehearsing. You run the risk of sounding bored, canned, and dull.

2. Meet the audience one on one

Welcoming your guests as they arrived gave you a chance to meet people one at a time. That enabled you to learn a bit about them. Finding out who your audience is and what it wants to learn helps to take the edge off your nervousness.

3. Breathe

Before you begin, take a moment to look at the audience, take a deep breath, and deliver your first sentence. For most presenters, this is the biggest hurdle. Once you've started, it gets much easier.

4. Make notes to yourself

On your cue cards or speaker's notes, add some words or symbols that will remind you to smile ☺, slow down ↓, speed up ↑, emphasize words, and so on. Create messages that will remind you to make your delivery as effective as possible. If you ignore these signals, you run the risk of losing the dramatic effects of the words in your presentation.

5. Focus on a friendly face

Look at your audience and watch for faces that appear receptive. They will be smiling and nodding their heads in agreement with your presentation points. When you feel like you are losing it, focus on these friendly faces.

g. HANDLING QUESTIONS

There will always be questions from your audience. Questions are a sign that participants are following along and are not sure how specific points fit into their personal agendas. Questions can be a sign of genuine interest in the topic and presentation. But not always.

Decide ahead of time whether you will answer questions as you go or save them until the end. Let your audience know what format you have chosen in your opening remarks. By encouraging questions throughout, you are inviting your audience to get actively involved, but some questions are used by audience members to put you on the spot or trap you into a position you may want to avoid.

How do you know what is behind the question? You don't. You must take all questions seriously and treat them in a similar manner. Be careful not to get sidetracked, and don't spend too much time with one questioner, ignoring the rest of the audience.

The general rule for answering questions is to restate the question to ensure you understand it properly, give your answer, then check back to make sure the participant is satisfied. For example, in answer to the question, "How many people have signed up for this new package?," you would —

(a) Restate the question: "Are you looking for the total number of new applicants since this package was introduced or the number of people involved in both the new and old package?"

(b) Answer the question: "Since you are interested in the new applicants only, I am pleased to report that, as of last Thursday, the number is 4,125."

(c) Check back: "Does that answer your question?"

The following represents some typical tough questions you may face from your audience.

1. The obscure point

Technical questions or those that deal with small, obscure points may be of little interest to the general audience and need not be answered in detail. However, you still need to let the audience know that you know the answer. Do this by giving a quick answer.

Giving a quick answer and inviting the questioner to stay behind later will maintain your level of credibility. "That's a good question. Paragraph three deals with an obscure law requiring full disclosure between spouses. If you want to talk

142

about in detail, perhaps we can get together after the presentation."

2. The loaded question

Some people get perverse pleasure out of asking questions that put you on the spot. It's a challenge we all could live without. The more controversial your topic, the tougher the question. For example, how would you answer a question such as, "Would you rather recommend a fund with a high rate of return than one specializing in investing in companies that will not harm the environment but with a lower rate of return?"

The solution is to take a deep breath and stay calm — even though it seems like no matter what you say, you will lose. Questions like this rarely come out of nowhere. Often, they relate to news stories or reports or simply to commonly held beliefs. By anticipating tough questions based on some of these reports and misconceptions, you can develop suitable answers ahead of time. A well-thought-out answer to the first question can sound as smooth as, "I think that both the right rates of return and dealing with companies that do as little damage to the planet as possible are both important. But it's not what I think that really matters. When we sit down, I will help you create a portfolio that is consistent with your personal values and objectives."

Remember, it never pays to lose your temper or get defensive.

3. I hadn't thought of that!

All the planning in the world will not guarantee that you will never face questions to which you do not know the answers. There are bound to be issues and points you had not considered beforehand. Rather than letting these questions upset the flow of your talk, consider them great learning opportunities.

Thank the participant for the question, acknowledge that you don't know the answer, and promise to get back to him or her once you get the answer. This allows you to maintain your credibility and gives you a reason for getting in touch with the participant after the presentation. Admitting truthfully that you do not know helps build credibility. It also can prevent you from giving a silly answer.

4. The parking lot

What if people raise issues that are important but not part of your presentation? It is tough to ignore such questions. One technique for handling these questions is called the parking lot technique. Rather than stopping your presentation and dealing with the question, offer to put it into the parking lot.

The parking lot is a helpful place for you to park those questions you would rather leave until later in your presentation. Be prepared for this with a flip chart or white board so the audience can see you write the question down. The parking lot can then be cleared at the end of your presentation. Just don't forget to deal with these questions or your audience will wonder why you ignored them.

5. Jumping the gun

There will always be people who want to rush ahead and get into points long before you are ready to discuss them. There may be things you had planned to deal with later in the presentation or that you have simply forgotten. With the latter, the parking lot technique works well.

With the former, use the quick answer technique. For example, you might say, "The quick answer is that they come in three sizes, but I will get into all the options later in this presentation."

Always be respectful of your audience. Even if you have already answered the question, answer it again, though this time more briefly. Never say, "I already answered that."

If you have decided to handle questions at the end of the seminar, be sure to wrap up your presentation by repeating the main points after the last question has been asked. Don't let your seminar end with a question from the audience. Instead, close with something thought-provoking and then thank everyone for attending.

h. HANDLING THE TROUBLEMAKERS

Every presenter dreads hecklers and troublemakers. These are people who seem bent on wreaking havoc on the presentation. Some do it on purpose and some do it unconsciously, without a hidden agenda.

Remain cool; don't get defensive. Try to handle the situation quickly and efficiently. Five of the typical workshop troublemakers you may encounter are the skeptic, the local genius, the break-in artist, the socialite, and the questioner.

1. The skeptic

The most vocal of the skeptics utter such words as "Oh, yeah!" or "Give me a break!" Skepticism this obvious is rare, but it still happens. More often you will hear a skeptic asking, "How do you really know it works that way?" or "Is your source an independent body?"

Skeptics aren't a bad element in the group. If fact, they often mirror a thought that others have but won't vocalize. Listen to the skeptic carefully. Clarify the comment so you can be sure you understood it and offer some other proof.

2. The local genius

There is always someone who knows everything about everything. Such a person will continue throughout the group to offer additional proof, comment on his or her own experience, and ask irrelevant queries. Some of what the local genius says can be helpful, but some can question your credibility. Often the person taking on the role of local genius has a strong need for recognition.

You can handle the local genius by thanking him or her for the input and making sure you don't ask for too much additional information. If you find you get stuck and there is very little audience participation, the local genius can then be called on again to voice opinions.

3. The break-in artist

You may encounter the participant who is constantly breaking into conversations: both yours and other participants'. If someone starts a sentence, the break-in artist is there to finish it. Start some new point, and the break-in artist has some comment to make. Often the break-in artist will interpret for the audience. "What I think Mr. Morris is trying to say is . . ."

With this type of troublemaker, avoid eye contact and minimize the comments he or she makes. If the person continues, you can always say, "Thank you Mr. Talker, some of your comments have been very helpful to all of us. I would like to hear what some of the rest of the group thinks about the matter."

4. The socialite

Watch out the socialite. This type of troublemaker jumps in and out of his or her chair. He or she leaves the room to use the telephone, talks to neighbors, and generally bothers others who are trying to concentrate.

There is very little you can do to stop the socialite from jumping up and running in and out of the room except to give the group a friendly reminder of when the break will be. When the socialite is engaged in conversation, you can simply say, "I would appreciate if we could handle one question at a time so you can all benefit from some of the experiences being shared by the audience."

5. The questioner

You have already learned how to handle some of the questions you will get from the audience. However, you may encounter the person who asks questions nonstop. Every point becomes lost in a barrage of questions. Some of these questions can be so detailed that very few of the other participants really care to hear the answer.

One way of handling this type of person is to ask the questioner to let some other people share their questions. Or you might say, "You seem to have a real interest in how this works and many good questions. Why don't you and I get together right after this presentation so I can give you the individual attention you deserve?"

i. HANDOUT MATERIALS

As discussed in chapter 3, many presenters give participants copies of transparencies or detailed notes which are helpful during the presentation. Sometimes, however, a take-home package is more effective. Giving participants materials after the presentation is over helps keep them focused on you during the presentation rather than on the paper in front of them.

If you are providing a take-home package, before the seminar begins, ensure that each participant has paper and pen to jot down notes. Tell participants that they will be getting detailed material at the end of the seminar.

j. USING AUDIO AND VISUAL AIDS EFFECTIVELY

Visual aids can have a huge impact on the lasting impression of your seminar. Research on the impact of visuals on memory retention has shown that after three days, people will remember only 10% of what they heard, 20% of what they saw, but 65% of information involving both sight and sound.

Visual aids can reinforce key points in your presentation and help clarify complicated or detailed information. By breaking up your presentation with visual aids, you keep the attention of your audience and add variety and professionalism to the presentation.

A word of warning, however: use visual aids to enhance your presentation, not replace it. Simplicity is often more effective than high tech. Don't get caught up in highly elaborate state-of-the-art technology unless that's your topic. (See chapter 3 for more on the advantages and disadvantages to using various audiovisual equipment.)

8
WORKING THE ROOM

The big event has finally arrived, and people are starting to fill up the room. You now assume your next role, that of host. As the host, you have a number of tasks: to meet people at the door, assure that their needs are taken care of, network during breaks and at the end of the seminar, send your guests away with a good feeling. All this must be accomplished with an air of grace and confidence so your guests will go home with a positive impression of you and your business. The secret to accomplishing this task is known to every Boy Scout: be prepared.

a. GREETING PEOPLE AT THE DOOR

Greeting people at the door requires more than waiting anxiously for people to arrive and hoping for the best. It is a carefully thought-out activity and if handled correctly, is the difference between a successful event and a failure.

A proper greeting puts your guests at ease so everything else that follows will go more smoothly. If guests start off being uncomfortable, they are likely to be less receptive and often more skeptical, and it will be harder to persuade them to do business with you. The first step in a proper greeting is to make the right first impression.

1. First impressions

First impressions are lasting. We have all seen people standing to one side of the room looking nervous, uninterested, bored, preoccupied, or aloof. What is your impression of these people? Negative, I imagine.

149

The right impression sends the message to your guests that you are pleased to see them and that they are special to you. Building rapport is how you ensure they have a good first impression of you; this begins the moment your guests walk in and see you.

To project the enthusiasm, energy, interest, and willingness to serve that will make guests feel welcome, you need to feel enthusiasm for the job at hand and demonstrate interest in your guests and their problems. Here are a few simple do's and don'ts to help you make the right first impression.

(a) Do's

- *Come rested.* Finish all your planning ahead of time so you can be rested and alert during the seminar. Looking tired and bored is not going to get you any business.

- *Dress comfortably and professionally.* New shoes or tight-fitting clothes are uncomfortable to wear and will affect your overall performance. The key word is professional. People want to do business with people who "look the part." So, wear clothes that project the right image. If you are in doubt, a little more formal is always better than being too casual. For men, formal can be as simple as wearing a tie. For women, it is wearing a skirt rather than pants.

- *Treat everyone equally and give them 100% of your attention.* You never know where tomorrow's business is coming from. Everyone at your seminar deserves equal treatment. Everyone, from the facility's service people to your guests, requires your best manners. Don't forget that people notice the way you treat others.

- *Maintain eye contact.* Have you ever talked with people who couldn't look you in the eye? They gaze with fascination at the floor, wall, or ceiling, anywhere but in your eyes. In some cultures, direct eye contact is considered inappropriate, but for most situations in the Western world, people would rather deal with people who look at them. Direct eye contact tells people you are interested and you are listening.

(b) Don'ts

- *Hand out business cards.* Unless you are specifically asked for your business card, save it until later. A warm, firm handshake beats exchanging business cards when you greet people at the door.

- *Be a gender genius.* A genius is someone who can focus all his or her attention on one thing while blocking out the rest of the world. That's okay if you are Albert Einstein. A gender genius, on the other hand, spends all his or her time talking to one guest because he or she wrongfully assumes that one sex is the decision-maker and the other is not.

- *Be a shark.* We have all experienced the lean and hungry look of the sharks. They are those smooth operators with cold, calculating eyes waiting to gobble you up. In the movie *Jaws*, sharks are described as mindless eating machines. Don't view your event as a tank filled with unsuspecting fish who will fall victim to their feeding frenzy.

- *Ignore your guests.* You're the host. Your job is to ensure that each person is looked after. When you're welcoming guests, don't get stuck in an extended conversation with one person and ignore everyone else. Spread your time evenly so that everyone is comfortable.

- *Smoke.* More and more, people are being turned off by the smell and hazards of secondhand smoke. If you smoke, leave it until later when you will not run the risk of offending anyone.

- *Put your hands in your pockets.* If you feel a bit apprehensive about meeting many people, that's understandable. But standing around with your hands in your pockets is uninviting and gives the impression you are bored and uninterested. Keep your hands at your sides and be ready to shake hands as each person arrives.

2. A well-rehearsed welcome

To achieve maximum effectiveness with your welcome statement, you should consider a touch of planned spontaneity. While this sounds like an oxymoron, on a closer look it may make some sense.

Your greeting should be well planned, giving you an opportunity to develop a message that feels most comfortable to you. Good networkers don't leave things to chance. The beauty of planning ahead is that your greeting flows so well, it sounds as if you had created it spontaneously.

A good greeting should take less than two minutes and involve four steps: making the introduction, tending to personal needs, creating a positive mood, and disengaging. Here is an excellent opportunity to begin to develop rapport with your guests. Let's examine each part individually.

(a) Make the introduction

Most of us are used to extending our hand in friendship when greeting someone, as well as when departing. Shaking hands is an internationally accepted way of saying hello and goodbye. However, there can be some hidden dangers with handshakers who have not mastered the art. Perhaps you have experienced some of these handshakers in your travels:

- *Peter Pumper.* Peter has a good handshake. The problem is that he doesn't know when to let go. Peter will hang on and, with a hand motion similar to what you might use to pump water out of a well, Peter pumps your hand.

- *Paul the pulverizer.* You've met Paul. He is the handshaker with a grip like a vice. As Paul shakes your hand, you can feel the bones in your hand disintegrating. The more you try to get out of Paul's grip, the harder he holds on.

- *Limp Larry.* Larry has a handshake you can barely feel. His hand feels like it will break if you squeeze too hard. It leaves you wondering if Larry has enough energy to lift that poor hand away from yours.

- *The wet fish.* The name says it all. After receiving this handshake, you are often left wanting to get to the nearest sink to scrub your hands.

People around the world have developed variations to their handshake greeting, but for the most part, a firm, short handshake will suffice. If your guests are from cultures other than Western, a little reading ahead of time will give you some clues about how to greet them appropriately.

Your handshake should be accompanied by a few words that tell your guest who you are. It provides an opportunity to say a few sincere words that express your delight at having him or her attend. It goes something like this: "Hi, my name is Barbara Siskind, and I am delighted that you are able to attend today's seminar."

(b) Tend to personal needs

As a good host, you don't want to leave your guest in the lurch. He or she may have a coat to check; if the weather is hot, he or she may want a cool drink; or if the guest has traveled a long way, he or she may need a washroom. Be sensitive to your guest's needs and address them quickly:

- "Let me hang your coat up for you."

- "If you need to freshen up, the washrooms are over there."

- "Let me show you where the refreshments are."

This is also your opportunity to remind your guest of the logistics of the event. Put your guest's mind at ease by saying something like, "We will be starting at seven o'clock. There are no reserved seats, but if you have a seating preference, I can lean those chairs forward so they will be saved for you."

(c) Create a mood

As your guests begin to fill the room, they will probably stay by themselves or with the people they came with. Your seminar is an educational event, but it can also provide your guests with an opportunity to build their networks. You can play an important role in their networking.

If you have preregistered your guests, you already have some general information about them, such as where they work, what they do, where they live, and so on. This is good basic information that you can use to help your guests mingle. As your guests arrive, rather than leaving them alone with a drink in their hands, find other guests for them to talk to. All good hosts do this. Take the information you learned before the event and see if there are opportunities for you to get people talking among themselves. For example, "I'd like you to meet Bill. Bill is also involved in junior hockey, and you might find that you know people in common" or "I'd like you to meet the Smiths. They are new in town."

(d) Disengage quickly

Don't make the mistake of spending too much time with some people, while ignoring others. You are there to greet everyone. Once you have set the mood, disengage and move on to the next guest: "I hope you enjoy tonight's program, and I hope we will get a chance to talk at the break."

b. NETWORKING

During seminar breaks, you are faced with a networking challenge. Your guests have been exposed to half of the program and will likely have some questions. The break gives you an opportunity to speak to some of your guests individually, get some feedback, find out if their needs are being met, and arrange for some personal follow-up. Your job is to work the room effectively so one person does not monopolize all your time. You want to make contact with as many guests as possible.

In networking, as in sports or the theater, it's the performance that counts. When you think of networking, what comes to your mind? For many people, networking is a terrifying word which conjures up images of meeting strangers in uncomfortable situations, waiting to break into conversations while people are engaged with others, sweaty palms, and nervous stomachs. Networking, like spinach, is one of those things we all know is good for us but that we tend to avoid.

Whether you like it or not, the success of meeting your seminar objectives depends on executing good networking skills. You are on stage and you will be judged by your performance. It's show time. You have begun the process in the welcome and reinforced it during the seminar, whether you are the speaker or the master of ceremonies. This is your chance to take that first impression the next step.

According to Barry Siskind in his book *Making Contact*, published by Macmillan Canada, networking is like a play with three acts. Each act has its own rationale and therefore must be learned separately.

Act One involves engaging people in conversation. Approaching guests can be uncomfortable. You may feel inhibited, afraid of appearing pushy. Or by coming on too strong, you may turn people off. For many, the art of engaging requires the greatest personal risk.

Act Two is called net-chat. In net-chat, you try to uncover some new information about your guest in as short a time as possible. You do this by taking a relaxed approach, a give-and-take approach, where you ask open questions while giving information back to your guest.

Act Three is the disengagement. One common mistake is spending too much time with too few people. The break is short, and you won't be maximizing opportunities if you can't end the encounter when you want to.

1. Act One: The approach

Approaching your guests and beginning a meaningful but short conversation can be the most difficult step in the process. Without an effective engagement, nothing else happens. I have attended events where guests either gather in comfortable cliques or stand by the wall or bar until the break ends. Your job as the host and an effective networker is to approach as many guests as possible, whether they are already engaged in conversation or not.

The principles of an effective approach are honesty and simplicity. If you are anything but honest, your nonverbal or paraverbal behavior will betray you. And as for simplicity, like everything else in life, you can overcomplicate things. Remember the KISS rule: keep it simple, stupid.

One common mistake networkers make is to make eye contact and say "Hi," with absolutely no idea of where to go from there. The problem of the simple hello is that most people respond with a smile and say "Hi" back, leaving an uncomfortable silence. On the other hand, some overbearing people will start talking about themselves and never attempt to learn anything about the people they have approached.

Why is approaching guests difficult? Because approaching strangers involves the unknown. Will they be receptive? Will they want to talk to me? Will they think I look foolish? What if I'm asked a question that I can't answer? What if they haven't enjoyed the seminar? What if I forgot something and they are angry with me?

You can hang back and wait for people to approach you, and because you are the host of the event, a certain number of guests will. But by taking a reactive rather than proactive approach, you will be missing opportunities. Many people are just as uncomfortable networking as you are, so take a deep breath and begin working the room.

A good approach will create the right impression and get you and the other person talking. The best way to get your guest talking is by asking questions. Try to ask questions that focus on positive things that are nonthreatening, easy to answer, and open ended. The best questions are ones that relate to the seminar. Here are some approach questions I have used:

- How did you first learn about tonight's seminar?

- What topics are most helpful to you?

- How do you see this information fitting into your plans?

- How does today's seminar compare with others you've attended?

Think about some questions you could ask comfortably and honestly at your next seminar.

2. Act Two: Net-chat

Once you have broken the ice, the next step is to engage in meaningful conversation. Your goal is to meet as many people as possible in the short time you have. There is no time for idle chitchat. Your main objective is to find out how your guest fits into your needs. You want to capture your guest's attention and whet your guest's appetite so that he or she wants to carry on a short conversation.

Think of net-chat as an opportunity to balance every bit of information you receive with information you are willing to share. While you are gathering information, you must be willing to share information. Networking is not a one-way process. To keep information flowing, you must do your part. Sharing information does not mean taking advantage of the opportunity to pitch, rather, it is a gentle opportunity for you to reveal information about yourself, your company, and your products or services that may fit your guest's needs. Personal information is quite appropriate. This can consist of your experiences or success stories. Avoid the hard sell.

The first step to your net-chat is to develop questions that will help you better understand your guest's interests. Here are some examples:

- What areas of alternative medicine are you interested in?

- What amenities would you like in a retirement community?

- What is your goal after finishing your formal education?

The next step is to determine how the information you have uncovered fits into your guest's future plans and, more important, do you play a role in these plans? For example, you could ask these questions:

- Are you interested in looking at a new dietary supplement?

- Have you found these amenities in the retirement communities you have visited?

- Have you found courses that can teach you these things?

3. Act Three: The disengagement

Once you have worked your way through the net-chat process and have identified your guest's future needs, it's time to disengage and move on. Spending extra time with one person is unproductive. Remember, you have hosted a seminar as an opportunity to meet as many people as possible; if you are stuck talking to only one or two people during the break, you are not using your time properly.

At prospecting seminars, I have repeatedly seen situations where the host does not disengage. The host qualifies a guest and develops real rapport. Perhaps the guest is fun and easy to talk to and the host doesn't want to disengage. Or perhaps the host qualifies the guest, sees a lot of potential, but continues to talk because he or she doesn't know how to break off the conversation without appearing rude.

Both cases require the skill of disengaging if you are going to make the most of your seminar. If in doubt, focus on your objective for holding the seminar in the first place. This is a constant reminder that should help keep you on track and will propel you into disengaging action.

The trick to disengaging properly is to break off the conversation politely, leaving your guest with a positive feeling about you. It is also a time to confirm any future plans. These plans may be concrete, such as setting up an appointment or a time to telephone, or a promise to send further information, or they may be open-ended plans — a promise to get together at some future date, or merely the expression of the hope of meeting again later.

Disengaging need not be difficult. It is a natural conclusion to a mutually rewarding conversation. You have presented yourself as someone willing to share some time, ideas, and solutions.

If you want to learn how to disengage correctly, listen to children. Children know how to disengage simply and honestly: "I have to go home now; see you tomorrow." As a lesson on disengaging in an adult world, take a moment and reflect on the simplicity with which children handle the same task.

Here are examples of disengagement lines I have used. Use these to stimulate your own creativity and develop exit lines that suit your personality and purposes.

When you have arranged a later meeting:

> "It has been great chatting with you. I would like to spend more time discussing this, but with everyone leaving, we are bound to be interrupted. Can I call you next week to set up a time when we can talk?"

or

> "Thank you for coming this evening. I'm looking forward to lunching with you next Wednesday."

When you do not have a specific follow-up:

> "Thank you for coming. I hope you picked up some new ideas."

or

> "It was good to meet you. If you have any questions in the future, please do not hesitate to call me."

Take the time to develop a few disengagement lines that you can use comfortably. You have put a lot of time and effort into this seminar. When working the room, always keep your goals in mind, and practice the skills of approaching, net-chat, and disengaging. The more you practice, the better you will be at them. Be patient, and don't worry about making mistakes.

c. AFTER THE SEMINAR

When the seminar is over, some people will leave quickly, while others will linger to speak to the guest speaker, ask you questions, or network with other guests. Do not assume that those who leave quickly did not enjoy or benefit from the seminar. There are many reasons they will leave immediately: they may have other engagements, they may be tired after a long day at the office, they have to pick up their kids, or they may be worried about driving if the weather is bad.

Your job is to talk to as many of these remaining guests as possible. You want to accomplish three things as they leave: answer their questions, thank them for attending, and leave them with a positive feeling.

1. Answer your guests' questions

You want to answer your guests' questions, but you must answer the right questions. The worst thing is to assume you have understood a question and proceed to give an answer that has nothing to do with the query. Good listeners answer questions with questions to confirm what they have heard. A simple clarifying question often prevents you from going off on a tangent. Section **g.** in the previous chapter discusses ways to clarify questions.

A guest who has stayed to speak with you after the seminar has ended may have done so in order to go into detail about his or her specific situation. If this is the case, stop the guest periodically while he or she is explaining a situation by saying, "Let me make sure I have got this straight. You need to see if there is an applicability of the information you just heard to . . ." or "Let me see if I have this right so far. You need . . ."

After the guest has finished, it is helpful for you to summarize by saying something like, "Okay, let me see if I understand. You said . . . . Is that right?" This kind of clarifying helps you avoid the embarrassing and costly mistake of answering the wrong questions and coming across as either arrogant or uninformed.

You also need to acknowledge the validity of your guests' questions. You are the expert, and sometimes people feel intimidated asking questions. Often this is why they have waited until the end of the seminar to ask their questions rather than asking them during the question-and-answer period.

Every question, no matter how mundane to you, is valid. The way you treat it is vital. Letting your guest know that the question is important takes the edge off. You accomplish this by a simple, "That's a really good question" or "I am glad you brought that up" or "I have met other people who have also been concerned about that."

When you are asked a question, make your answer short, concise, and simple. You have already shown that you have some expertise in this area. Urge your guest to set up an appointment with you to explore the issue further. Take the initiative and say, "There is more to your question than we can deal with here. Why don't we schedule a meeting to discuss how my services can meet your specific needs. How does some time next week sound?"

2. Thank your guests for attending

Try to stop each guest for a moment to thank him or her for attending. As a gracious host, you want to make sure that your guests know that you appreciate the effort they put into making your seminar a success. A simple thank-you is a powerful tool. Your guests have busy lives and lots of ways to spend their spare time. They chose your seminar, and it is important to let them know you appreciate the choice. Simply say, "Thank you for taking the time to come out tonight."

3. Leave your guests with a good feeling about you

The success of an event is often attributed to looking after the little things. This last step is like the icing on the cake. You conducted the seminar for a large audience, so you need to make sure that each guest feels that he or she was an important part of the event. Your last remark should be sincere and delivered with direct eye contact. "I really enjoyed meeting you" or "I hope our paths cross again" or "I am looking forward to meeting you next week." Leave your guests with a positive feeling about you by treating them as individuals and not just part of the mass audience.

d. CONSIDERING CULTURAL DIFFERENCES

As the world gets smaller — thanks to technology — one of your biggest challenges will be dealing with different cultures. Every culture has its own words, gestures, and approaches to people and experiences. Learning another culture perfectly is impossible unless you are prepared to live in that culture for years, but you still can develop a cultural sensitivity and become aware of the role cultural differences play in how people act in various situations.

Watching and learning about various cultures can be rewarding and fascinating. There are countless numbers of books offering advice on things to do and things to avoid. It is well worth your time to do a bit of research if you will be dealing in your seminars with people from different cultures.

One of the common pitfalls is to make generalizations about how people act in certain situations. Without an in-depth understanding of a certain culture, you might assume certain things. However, culture is complicated. You cannot simply conclude that all people in a country act and think the same. Here are three ways of dealing with cultural differences:

(a) *Understand your audience makeup.* When you began to plan your seminar, you targeted a particular demographic group. Within this group will be a number of cultures. Finding out the predominate cultures is a matter of knowing your audience. Find out during preregistration who will be attending your seminar.

(b) *Get the big picture.* A number of excellent books are available that deal with cultural differences. A few are listed in Appendix 2. Read about the cultures you are interested in and you will learn "the big picture."

163

Having this information will help you avoid some of the obvious pitfalls.

(c) Use your sense of humor

If you have done your best and still make a mistake, remember that dealing with cultural differences is a two-way street. Your guests will be trying to adjust to your culture just as you are trying to adjust to theirs. If you make a mistake, admit it openly, keep your sense of humor, and with the greatest respect, say, "I hope I didn't offend you. Thank you for correcting me. I am just learning about your culture, and you have now taught me one more thing."

9
EVALUATION AND FOLLOW-UP

After the seminar is over, two jobs still remain: evaluation and follow-up. Yet these important steps are often neglected, relegated to the realm of chance rather than good planning.

When I ask people how their seminars went, I typically get answers such as, "It was great" or "It went okay" or, at the other extreme, "I didn't get anything out of it" or "It was a waste of time." These are vague answers that do not produce any constructive results.

Evaluation and follow-up are as crucial to your seminar planning as anything else covered in this book. Both evaluation and follow-up are time-consuming and detailed, requiring your attention long before the seminar takes place so that they can be completed quickly and accurately once the seminar is over.

The higher the quality of information you gather, the better you can plan future events. You can build on your strengths and eliminate those elements that were costly and unproductive.

a. EVALUATION

By evaluating every aspect of your seminar, you gain valuable information for planning future seminars. You need to evaluate three crucial areas: your sales objectives, your communication objectives, and your seminar planning.

165

1. Your sales objectives

Sales objectives are foremost for most seminars. However, sales objectives are not limited to your products or services. Sales objectives can also include your ability to persuade participants to help you achieve your goals — whether through direct sales, leads for future business, support from an association, or initiation of a change in attitude. In chapter 2, you set out your sales objectives in detail. Now you have the opportunity to measure your success.

Sales objectives are often the easiest objectives to measure. They are the total number of appointments, leads, or direct sales you received as a result of the seminar. But you need to examine them from two points of view. You need to know if the volume of business you received justified the cost of the seminar, and you need to develop benchmarks for future marketing expenditures. The more seminars you conduct, the better you will be able to predict your results.

Mark Carriere, director of marketing at Carriage Hills Resort, a vacation property in Ontario, is an active user of seminars to market the property. His example shows how you can use evaluation to improve your marketing strategy.

Carriere takes a two-pronged approach. First, he offers prospects an opportunity to attend a 90-minute information seminar. Prospects each receive a small gift such as a gift certificate or dinner at a nice restaurant as an incentive to attend. After years of conducting these seminars, Carriere knows that about 70% of those who say they will come actually do show up. His sales and support staff attend these information sessions and mingle with attendees.

The next stage is to get the serious prospects to visit the property. This involves a larger incentive. Carriage Hills offers prospects an opportunity to visit the property and stay overnight — a $179 value for a nominal fee of $30. Carriere charges this small fee because many people perceive that if something is free, it is worthless: "If there is very little value, the no-show rate is high." By charging the small fee, he eliminates 50% of those who attended the introductory session.

About 70% of those committed to this second phase of overnighting at Carriage Hills will show up for a personalized, guided discovery tour to visit the site for a more detailed presentation. The closing rate for those visiting the site is between 12% and 15%. Here is a summary of Carriere's success rate:

Number of participants confirmed to the initial seminar:	100	
Number who will show up:	70	(70%)
Number who will commit to phase two:	35	(50%)
Number who will show up:	25	(70%)
Closes:	4	(15%)

Carriere's success rate varies, depending on whether prospects came through cold calls or referrals. If through referrals, the success rate can be as high as 40%. Ninety percent of people who come make up their minds while they are there; very few come back for a second look. Carriere estimates that it costs between $150 and $300 for every prospect delivered. At the end of each prospecting seminar, he knows whether he has met his sales objective.

Raymond Aaron, principal of the Raymond Aaron Group which runs seminars across Canada and the United States, offers another example. Aaron presents an introductory 90-minute seminar where he talks about buying real estate with almost no money down. Aaron's objective is to sell tapes and books and enroll people in longer courses.

Aaron has two benchmarks for the success of the seminar: *dollars per head* and *percentage closing. Dollars per head* is the total dollar value of on-the-spot sales divided by the number of participants:

$$\frac{\text{Dollar value of on–the–spot sales}}{\text{Number of participants}} = \text{Dollars per head}$$

Aaron is satisfied if he can collect $50 per head selling tapes, books, and course enrollments. Therefore, if he is targeting 50 people, he expects to gross $2,500 ($50 x 50) at the seminar.

This does not mean that everyone bought products. Nor does it indicate the "quality" of participants, which is a quantitative measure. Theoretically, one person could spend $2,500 and 49 people could spend nothing. This is why Aaron uses a second, more qualitative benchmark.

Percentage closing is the number of sales divided by the number of participants:

$$\frac{\text{Number of sales}}{\text{Number of participants}} = \text{Percentage closing}$$

For Aaron, percentage closing should be 10% or greater; if fewer than 10% of attendees bought something, his seminar has not been successful because of the quality of participants.

You can play with the numbers in a variety ways, but you must be careful. For example, you can increase the percentage closing by offering lower-priced products, but this affects the dollars per head number. Conversely, if you increase your price points, you jeopardize the percentage closing. Finding the right balance is the trick. This comes with time and experience, and every situation is different. If you evaluate your results properly using these two methods, you will in time develop realistic targets for your prospecting seminars.

2. Your communication objectives

Communication objectives are longer term than your sales objectives. They are those activities that bring in future business but not necessarily immediate results. Communication objectives are more abstract and for that reason, more difficult to measure than sales objectives. But they are just as important to your long-term growth and should not be ignored.

Communication objectives fall into two broad categories: long-term action and public relations.

(a) Long-term action

Harry Plack, a Baltimore-based management consultant, says that when evaluating a prospecting seminar, you need to look at the sales cycle of your products or services. Your sales cycle depends on the products or services you are offering, the timeliness of your seminar, and the maturity of the products in the marketplace.

The simple way to evaluate your sales cycle is to ask yourself the question, "How long is it, on average, from when I meet a prospect until he or she makes a commitment?" This can be a tough question because every interaction you have is different. However, if you can think in average terms, your task will be easier.

If you respond by saying that it takes two to four months for people to commit, your average is three months. Having calculated this, you may not expect to evaluate the results until three months, six months, or even a year has passed.

(b) Public relations

Once you begin to promote your seminar, your business will be receiving long-term benefits that may be difficult to measure. In chapter 4, I discussed the preparation of a media release to help promote your seminar. If you were lucky, you received some immediate coverage, but you did not waste your efforts on those who did not respond.

Often, the media keep files on interesting people or topics that they refer to from time to time as sources for future stories. If you have done your job well, you could gain the extra benefit of being the person they call on for quotations, comments, and information. Remember that the media works to tight deadlines; if they have trouble getting in touch with you, they will lose interest and move on to other prospects.

Evaluating your communication objectives requires good record keeping. It is a matter of calculating your return of investment. Look at what you spent in hard dollars and compare these expenses with both your long- and short-term results. To measure this, each time you get a call from a warm lead or someone from the media, ask where that person learned of you. If the person refers to a specific seminar, record this as another point for your prospecting seminar. With experience, you will be able to guesstimate with reasonable accuracy the short- and long-term results of your seminar.

3. Your seminar planning

You have put much effort into planning the seminar, but you need to know what worked and what didn't. There is always room for improvement. To ensure that you analyze your efforts properly, a formal seminar evaluation is in order. This evaluation serves two purposes. First, many decisions involved in planning your seminar were likely based on intuition. There is nothing wrong with using intuition to plan a seminar, but on closer examination you may find some things worked better than others and some things did not work at all.

Recently, I spoke to a planner who chose a community center for her seminar. It seemed like a good idea because it was convenient, not too expensive, and the center was under local pressure to increase business. She thought she would receive a positive response from the community for using the facility. Unfortunately, the center did not have the labor necessary to handle last-minute problems. All her good intentions went out the window because of the facility's logistic problems. However, on the written evaluations, two participants commented that they were glad she chose to use the facility. Some of the other participants made negative comments.

Without conducting a formal evaluation, you may tend to block out the negative comments and focus only on the positive ones. As well, some people's comments may carry more weight with you than others'. Often, we listen to the vocal minority and ignore the silent majority. In either case, to get good information, you need to prepare a proper written evaluation.

The second reason for evaluating the seminar is so that you can report to your sponsors. In chapter 5, we discussed ways your sponsors will evaluate the effectiveness of your seminar and how well it fit into their marketing plans. Your sponsors are entitled to a postseminar report that will give them enough information to evaluate their support properly.

I recommend evaluating your seminar throughout the planning process. According to Robert G. Simerly, author of *Planning and Marketing Conferences and Workshops* published by Jossey-Bass publishers, there are two different types of evaluation. Formative evaluations are done before and during the seminar to help formulate ideas and improve the program. Summative evaluation takes place at the end and summarizes the reactions of the participants.

A formative evaluation recognizes that you do not need to wait until the seminar is over to know if you are on track. Good planners capitalize on their preseminar contacts to give them valuable information. You can talk to participants as they register to gather important information. In addition, you may also want to talk to those you have invited but who do not register. Initially, you might telephone invitees to confirm that they received their invitations and to ask them if they plan to attend. If they say no, you can ask why not.

You and your staff should have a checklist beside the telephone so that you are prepared with appropriate questions when you contact invitees. Here are some appropriate questions.

For attendees:

- What are you hoping to learn?
- How do you think you will use this information?
- Is the timing of the seminar convenient for you?
- Is there someone you would like to bring to the seminar?
- Do you have any dietary restrictions?
- Do you have any special needs?
- Do you need directions to the facility?
- Have you heard of our guest speaker before?
- How did you hear about the seminar?

For nonattendees:

- Why can't you attend?
- Are you interested in attending future seminars?
- Can we keep you on our mailing list?
- What topics would be helpful to you?
- When would be the best time for you to attend a seminar?
- Where should we hold our future seminars?
- Which newspaper do you read most often?
- Which television station do you watch most often?
- Which radio station do you listen to most often?
- How long should the seminars be?
- Is there anyone else we should add to our mailing list?

Once the seminar is over, you have another chance to gather information with a summation evaluation. Seminar participants are used to completing a postworkshop evaluation. It is their chance to let you know how you did. Your evaluation is more than a smile sheet — an opportunity for people to tell you all the good things you did. It is an opportunity for them to give you honest opinions on all aspects of the seminar.

If you choose to ask participants to complete a postseminar evaluation, ask them to do it immediately after the seminar. The return rate is very low if you ask them to send the evaluations in later. If you can find a way to have participants complete it immediately, the information is current and therefore more reliable. I often arrange for thank-you gifts for participants. I ask each participant to hand in the evaluation in return for the gift. Small premiums such as pens, calendars, mugs, or tickets for a draw are effective.

You will find it easier to compile all the information if you ask quantitative questions. You can use a sliding scale of one to five, with five being "strongly agree" and one being "do not agree," or you can give choices such as "better than expected," "as expected," or "less than expected."

Qualitative data that are compiled from written comments are harder to measure but should still be collected. Consider asking questions such as "What did you like best?" and "What did you like least?"

Also leave space at the bottom of the evaluation for other comments. This encourages participants to add extra information that you may not have thought to ask for. The evaluation should not take more than a few minutes to complete.

Sample #6 is an example of a comment sheet you might want to use or adapt.

1. Overall evaluation (please circle the answer that best describes your response):

   a. Overall, how would you rate the seminar:

      Better than   As expected   Not as good as
      expected   expected

   b. Usefulness of the presentation:

      Very useful   Somewhat   Not useful at all
                     useful

   c. The presentation:

      Excellent   Good   Fair

   d. To what extent has your knowledge on the subject increased from attending the seminar?

      A lot   Somewhat   Not at all

2. What did you find most valuable in the seminar?

   _____

   _____

3. What would you have like to have heard in the seminar that you did not?

   _____

   _____

   _____

4. What action do you plan to take as a result of the information you received?

_____

_____

5. How did you hear about the program?

_____

_____

6. Are you interested in having someone call you to discuss this topic further?

Yes   No

(Office telephone) _____

(Home telephone) _____

7. Suggestions of other topics:

_____

_____

8. Other comments:

_____

_____

_____

If you know of other people who might be interested in attending this seminar in the future, please pass seminar information on to them, or give us their names and contact numbers, and we will gladly contact them.

b. FOLLOW-UP

The seminar is finally over. You did a great job and the participants were positive. You are also emotionally relieved now that all the planning and worrying is finally history. What's next? If you sit back, put up your feet, and wait for the calls or orders to come rushing in, you are wasting your time. Your ability to follow up with each participant will allow you to reap the real benefits of holding prospecting seminars.

According to Barry Siskind in his book *The Power of Exhibit Marketing* published by Self-Counsel Press, there are six elements to a good follow-up plan:

(a) Set realistic goals for the number of prospects you plan to meet.

(b) Design and use a follow-up system that makes recording and retrieval easy. There is a plethora of contact management systems on the market. You can use an electronic or manual system, whichever you are more comfortable with. Spend some time with your business products supplier or at the computer store and try out the various programs available to find the one that works best for you.

(c) Plan your follow-up system well ahead of the seminar, and have it ready to roll immediately. If you leave your follow-up planning until after the seminar, you are putting yourself at a disadvantage. You will certainly go after the hot leads right away, but without a good plan in place, you will be missing other valuable opportunities.

(d) Set deadlines for follow-up activities, and brief all staff involved in the seminar on the importance of meeting these deadlines. When you set deadlines, make them realistic. If you are too aggressive in your follow-up and your prospects are not ready, you will frustrate everyone. If you are too slack, you will lose business.

(e) Set up a system to record and review results of your follow-up program. Every contact with participants should be recorded. One important element to include in your system is the recording of anecdotal information. This is crucial to your long-term relationship with prospects. Everyone wants to be recognized for his or her individual qualities. Don't leave anything to your memory — write it down. All prospecting information should be in one central place or data base so everyone on your staff has access to pertinent information.

(f) Monitor your results. Your file could conceivably be open-ended, particularly when you consider your long-term communication objectives. Review the file at regular intervals, depending on how your business works and what makes most sense. You may consider doing this every 3, 6, or 12 months. At some point you will need to close the file and move on to others.

How you choose to follow up is a decision based on your style and schedule. You can use basic tools to give your follow-up some variety. You may consider adding a combination of telemarketing, direct mail, fax, and e-mail to your arsenal of tools.

1. Telemarketing

The objective of telemarketing is to make personal contact with the prospect. It is a great technique for those leads that require immediate follow-up. Telemarketing has developed a negative image because many telemarketing calls often occur just as people are about to start eating dinner. However, if handled properly, telemarketing can yield valuable results.

Here are some guidelines to good telemarketing.

(a) Make the calls yourself, or have people with a complete understanding of your products, services, and seminar objectives make the calls.

(b) Identify your company and mention the seminar. This lets the prospect know who is calling and it acts as a reminder in case he or she has forgotten your name.

(c) Set a telemarketing objective. Your reason for calling is to set up an appointment, get the order, ask for a pledge, or recruit volunteers. The first step in successful telemarketing is to understand clearly why you are making the call.

(d) Have a backup objective. If the prospect cannot meet your objective, try a backup. Some backup objectives are to arrange for a call at a specific time or to send additional information.

(e) If the prospect has questions that cannot be answered immediately, take notes and promise to get back to the prospect with the answer within 24 hours.

(f) Any promises made to the prospect should be recorded and acted on immediately.

(g) Record all the prospect's comments in your follow-up contact management system.

(h) Be friendly but persistent. People tend to move away from an obvious hard sell. If you can keep the call friendly and informative, you will have better results. It all starts with the first few words, as in this example:

"Hi, my name is Barbara, and we met at the "Change Your Life" seminar you attended last Tuesday. The reason for my call is to check back with you to find out if you got the information you were looking for and if there is anything else I can help you with."

2. Direct mail

A follow-up tool that is abused and misused can give that tool a bad reputation, and unsolicited mail is one such tool. However, if your mail-out piece is carefully thought-out and relevant to the recipient, it will be viewed correctly.

Direct mail works well with prospects who have expressed some long-term interest in your seminar or business. The objective of your direct mail is to keep reminding the recipients who you are and what you do. You are building rapport through the mail. If people see your name enough times and have a positive image of your products or services, the likelihood of them conducting business with you is greater than if you had not kept in touch at all.

Using direct mail involves a long-term commitment. Simply sending out one letter thanking participants for attending your seminar is not enough. The frequency of your mailings will depend on the products or services you have to offer and the availability of newsworthy items to send.

Your first direct-mail piece should be sent immediately after the seminar as a thank-you to prospects for attending, to reinforce the material they were exposed to at the seminar, and to leave the door open for future contact.

Further correspondence can be as creative as you like. In your subsequent letters, refrain from sending unsolicited brochures. They were not requested and will be viewed as junk mail. Look for interesting things to send: newspaper or magazine articles, announcements from suppliers, invitations to trade shows, and so on. Each time you send something to a prospect, record it in your contact management system.

By developing a keen sense of what is important to your prospects and what they are interested in learning about, you

179

are assured that your mail will be welcomed rather than rejected.

One friend of mine constantly scours newspapers for articles and announcements. He simply clips the article and attaches his business card with the handwritten message, "I thought you might be interested in this," and sends it to the prospect.

3. Fax

Just like the mail, faxes can also be perceived as junk. Recipients of junk faxes are quite vocal in their complaints because receiving unsolicited faxes often means an out-of-pocket expense for them. However, if you use the fax machine as a marketing tool properly, you can eliminate most problems.

The three best reasons to use a fax are to confirm, to add validity, and to remind.

(a) *To confirm.* Faxes are a great way to confirm the time and place of your seminar and any subsequent meetings. The information is received instantaneously and your transmission report is a confirmation that it has been received (if not by the prospect himself or herself, at least by the office).

(b) *To add validity.* Faxes can be used to inform participants about last-minute details about your seminar and pass on newsworthy information to them quickly after the seminar.

(c) *To remind.* Once again, you can use faxes to remind people to come to the seminar and, after the seminar, to reiterate to them what they heard. Some seminar planners prepare a fax outlining the salient points that were covered in the seminar and send them to all the participants immediately afterward. Their objective is two-fold: it gives them an excuse to make contact and participants often appreciate a quick summary of the program.

180

4. E-mail

The number of people who use e-mail is staggering and is growing by leaps and bounds. E-mail is a fast, easy way of keeping in touch with participants. It gives you a low-cost method of staying in touch and providing new information.

E-mail messages should not to be lengthy. A simple sentence outlining the facts you want to pass along is sufficient.

The disadvantage to e-mail is that you don't always know if the participant has read your message. You may know that the message was sent successfully, but you have no way of knowing how often the recipient accesses his or her e-mail. Your message could sit in the prospect's mailbox for a long time before being read.

10
CONCLUSION

Congratulations! You are now ready to organize a prospecting seminar. As you read through the various chapters in this book, you saw how an organized and well-planned approach takes some of the fright away from a daunting task. You learned the importance of setting objectives and the advantages of soliciting and working with sponsors. You learned how to cope with the overwhelming details of the logistics, market your seminar, work with a guest speaker, give the presentation yourself, work the room, and evaluate and follow up once the seminar is over.

This approach involves a lot of detail, but it is a valuable road map that will keep everything organized so that you won't miss important steps.

I have been organizing seminars for the past ten years and there is one more point I would like to share with you. I have worked with both experienced planners and neophyte seminar organizers, and I am often struck by how little fun these people have doing their jobs. Sure, there is a lot at stake and a lot to remember. However, unless there is some joy in what you do, what's the point?

Integrating prospecting seminars into your marketing mix can be a profitable addition to your business plans. The rewards are endless and that alone should make you feel good. But you also want your guests to enjoy themselves. Your attitude will rub off on them. If you are having a good time and are enjoying your work, this positive feeling will be reflected in your guests' attitudes.

However, the opposite is also true. If you treat the seminar as a tireless task and let everything upset you, your attitude will also be reflected in your guests' eyes.

So go out there and have some fun. You are taking on an interesting challenge and after it's all over, you will be able to take some time to give yourself a pat on the back.

I am very interested in hearing about your seminar plans. I would like to know what worked well and what pitfalls you encountered. You can reach me at:

> 16436 Shaw's Creek Road
> Terra Cotta, ON
> Canada L0P 1N0
> or via e-mail: itmc@ican.net.

APPENDIX 1

A POTPOURRI OF SEMINAR IDEAS

The number of different types of companies that have successfully used seminars as a marketing tool is truly amazing. In this appendix, I have gathered together an interesting mixture of success stories, provocative ideas, and helpful tips. The businesses, ranging from financial and medical services to real estate companies and retirement villages, have all found ways to use seminars creatively.

You can learn from their experiences, from how they handled their logistics and marketing to those little tricks that gave their seminars an edge and produced big rewards. Read these stories with your seminar in mind and you may find ideas that you can borrow to make your next seminar a smashing success.

Travel seminars

Demographically, there is a whole generation of seniors out there who are living longer, with more money and energy, looking for better ways to spend their retirement years. For many of them, travel has become a consuming passion.

Mary Mursell, the sales and marketing manager of Senior Tours Canada, constantly uses seminars to solicit new business. Each year, the five offices of her company run about 40 seminars, each office organizing its own. In larger urban centers, these seminars each attract as many as 300 attendees, while in smaller communities, attendance ranges between 50 and 80 attendees.

The presentations try to give the audience a personal experience by including photographs and testimonials from previous participants.

Mursell and her colleagues work with a tourist bureau as well as a local tour operator in the country they are promoting in the seminar. They also try to involve an airline.

A question-and-answer period supported by a video or slide show follows a 20-minute introduction. One of Mursell's staff members acts as master of ceremonies. Each seminar focuses on one destination, but staff members are available to discuss other tours.

The secondary objective of the seminar is public relations. Guests have an opportunity to meet other seniors who have traveled with the company before and who can pass on their positive experiences. It is a forum for Mursell and her colleagues to service their current client base as well as add names to their mailing list. It's a positive way to reinforce the message that they are more than just voices on the telephone.

Each seminar is planned five months in advance and publicized through the company's own mailing list and newsletter, as well as through advertisements in local papers. Figure #7 is an example of one such advertisement.

FIGURE #7
TRAVEL SEMINAR ADVERTISEMENT

SENIOR TOURS ADMISSION FREE

TRAVEL SEMINAR
GREECE

TORONTO ... SEPTEMBER 23, 2 - 4 p.m.
THE OLD MILL, 21 Old Mill Road

Videos, slides, Greek treats, plus *A CHANCE TO WIN A TRIP TO SUNNY GREECE.* To register please call us over the weekend or any day AFTER 5PM and leave your name, phone number & seminar date on our answering service.

416-322-1500
TOLL FREE
1-800-268-3492

Senior Tours

225 Eglinton Avenue West, Toronto, M4R 1A9

When asked about possible pitfalls, Mursell cautions seminar organizers to be very careful with audiovisual equipment. If your seminar relies on a slide or video program, make sure you have backup equipment. Double-check the videotape to be sure you don't have a video of Jamaica for your Alaskan cruise seminar. (It has been known to happen!)

Each seminar is more than a sales pitch. It provides an opportunity for participants to expand their levels of knowledge about places and events. For some, it is an opportunity to network with other people who share similar interests and who might eventually become travel companions.

Mursell always asks participants to complete a comment sheet which she uses as an entry form for a giveaway to ensure it is returned.

Family planning seminar: in-vitro fertilization

"The advancements in in-vitro fertilization techniques have been staggering. They provide a viable option for couples who in the past had very few options," says Judy Grant of the Pacific Fertility Centre, who runs six to eight seminars across North America each year.

The seminars disseminate information to participants who have been unsuccessful with other fertilization options. The audiences range in size from 50 to 300, depending on the location. Seminars consist of a one-hour presentation followed by a question-and-answer period. The speaker is a medical doctor who later works with couples who choose to become patients of the Centre.

"Even though this information is very personal, participants are quite candid and willing to share their concerns. There are no hecklers in the audience," says Grant. "They are very serious people looking for ways to increase their chances of getting pregnant and have come for answers."

Information includes the latest breakthroughs in the field, the various fertility options, and a description of the Centre and how it can help participants.

"The seminar is a very effective way of getting new patients into the Centre," says Grant. Although exact figures are not available, when Centre staff review their patient intake every six months to determine the source of new patients, they have found that seminars are one of the Centre's most effective marketing tools.

The Centre also advertises its service in newspapers, on radio, and on its Web site. Word-of-mouth referrals have also brought in new patients.

Retirement living seminars

Baby boomers and their parents have developed into a burgeoning market for specialized retirement-lifestyle accommodation. Marlene White, marketing manager of Lifestyle Retirement Communities, runs educational seminars as a public relations forum to encourage people to visit one of the company's buildings to take a personal look at what retirement living is all about. It is a very soft sell.

Participants register to hear a high-profile speaker. When they preregister, they are asked if they would like to have a tour of the facility. About one-quarter of the audience takes the tour.

"It is a long sales cycle for retirement living communities. People start to look at options five to ten years before they are ready to make a decision," says White. This type of marketing keeps the retirement community in the minds of the potential residents.

The seminar is also open to the potential clients' children, as they are usually actively involved in such decisions. To encourage this, the advertisement for the seminar reads, "Adults only, 65 and over (Youngsters 64 and under must be accompanied by an adult)." (See Figure #8.)

FIGURE #8
RETIREMENT LIVING SEMINAR ADVERTISEMENT

Adults Only
65 and Over
(Youngsters 64 and under
must be accompanied by an adult)

UPCOMING EVENTS FOR SENIORS

Beechwood Place
1500 Rathburn Rd. E., Mississauga

Dinah Christie's Smile Theatre presents 'Bandstand – The Dance Musical'
Enjoy an evening of nostalgic music. Refreshments and Door Prize.
Wednesday, December 3 – 7:30pm

'Harmony Show Band'
Music with a touch of Christmas. Refreshments and Door Prize.
Wednesday, December 17 – 7:30pm

Call Sylvia or Maryana (905) 238-0800 to reserve your place

Donway Place
8 The Donway East, Don Mills

'10th Anniversary Open House'
Come celebrate with us! Craft show, carollers, Santa and entertainment. Proceeds going to Toronto's Daily Bread Food Bank. Free poinsettia for those who participate in a tour. Refreshments & Free Admission. Saturday, December 13 – 10:00am - 3:30pm

'A Christmas Show'
Music for you featuring Eric James. Refreshments & Free Admission.
Friday, December 19 – 2:30m - 3:30pm

Call Pam or Rosemarie at (416) 445-7555 to reserve your place

Forest Hill Place
645 Castlefield Ave., Toronto

'The Real Theodore Herzl – The Legacy of Zionism'
Lecturer Selma Sage. Thursday, December 4 – 2:00pm

'Tea & Tours – Open House'
Forest Hill Place invites you to join us for tea and a tour.
Sunday, December 7 – 1:00-3:00pm

'Shalom Singers'
Thursday, December 11 – 2:00pm

Call Marlene or Karen at (416) 785-1511 to reserve your place

LIFESTYLE
Retirement Communities
A Subsidiary of London Life
Ask about our other locations in Burlington and Oakville.

Financial seminars

The financial industry regularly uses seminars as a marketing tool. You can easily find advertisements in your local newspaper for these seminars, which have titles such as "Worry Free Retirement," "What the Rich Do," and "Five Steps to Financial Independence."

Large companies (with large budgets) have the advantage of hiring prominent speakers or authors to draw large crowds. Their objective, in addition to generating leads, is to create corporate awareness. The success of these seminars is often based on audience size, and seminars attracting more than 300 people are not uncommon.

Promotion is generally through local newspapers, and registrations are usually taken through a national toll-free number. It is not unusual for these events to have budgets of $10,000 to $15,000.

But these large events may not be suitable for many independent financial planners, both in terms of time and cost. Because the financial sector is one of the most prominent users of prospecting seminars, the market for traditional topics and overused speakers is quickly becoming saturated.

I spoke to one financial planner who organizes three seminars each year during the peak retirement savings season (January to March). He asks one of his suppliers to provide a speaker and markets the program through invitations. After each seminar, all leads are followed up immediately by telemarketers, an essential step in an industry with stiff competition.

All this does not mean you should rule out prospecting seminars if you are in the financial services business. But to give your seminar an advantage over the competition, you need to develop an interesting hook, something that will differentiate yours from the rest.

Tracey Marshall, a financial planner with Security Financial Services and Investment in Brampton, Ontario, has found that interesting hook. Her business strategy is targeted to the female investor; to add an interesting spin, she partners with a fashion consultant to offer a seminar called "Wealth and Image." The presentation time is divided equally between Marshall and the fashion consultant.

Marshall holds the seminar twice a year. One seminar is supported by her local chamber of commerce while the other she supports herself. Invitations are mailed three weeks in advance to her clients and referrals. She gets additional exposure by distributing invitations at local networking meetings. Her objective is to attract 30 to 40 women to each seminar.

Specialized medical seminars: laser eye surgery

A new and revolutionary technique has been invented to help the 50 million people in the world who wear glasses — laser corrective surgery. Performed by highly trained doctors, laser surgery has become commonplace for those people wishing to throw away their glasses and contact lenses.

Years ago, the Canadian Medical Association frowned on doctors who advertised their services. That attitude prompted doctor Calvin Breslin of the Toronto Laser Sight Centre to begin a series of information seminars. Since he began offering seminars in 1990, attitudes toward such advertising have changed, but Breslin found seminars so successful that he continued to offer them every two weeks.

The purpose of the seminar is to explain laser sight surgery to large groups of people. Although Breslin provides free consultations in his office, many people attend the seminar first because they believe they won't feel pressured to make immediate decisions. Following the seminar, many participants wait about six months before returning for consultations and deciding whether to have the surgery.

FIGURE #9
LASER EYE SURGERY SEMINAR ADVERTISEMENT

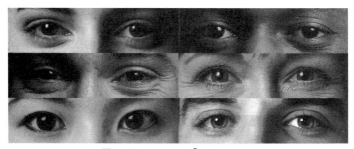

Join us for an eye-opening experience on laser vision correction

Free Educational Seminars

Laser vision correction of nearsightedness, farsightedness
and astigmatism using PRK and LASIK

Wednesday, September 17th and 24th • 7:00 p.m. - 8:00 p.m.

Toronto Laser Sight Centre

Seating is limited. Reserve your place today.

Laser vision correction has already improved the vision of close to one million people worldwide since 1987. Most patients are able to work, drive or play sports without always needing glasses or contacts after treatment. To learn more about laser vision correction for nearsightedness, farsightedness and astigmatism and to see if you are a candidate, please attend one of our free seminars. Call today to register or to receive more information.

1-800-243-EYES
www.lca-vision.com

TORONTO

LASER SIGHT
CENTRE

Wake up and see the world.℠

Toronto's member of the LCA-Vision Network (Nasdaq:LCAV)
Atria II • 2235 Sheppard Avenue E. • Suite 101 • Willowdale • (416) 492-3937

Results may vary by patient.

© LCA-Vision Inc.

Breslin says newspaper advertisements (see Figure #9, an example of one the advertisements Breslin uses) for his seminar accomplish three things: they bring people to the seminar, they give readers a telephone contact (his toll-free number if they want information), and they provide people with an opportunity to visit the Centre's Web page. All responses are monitored to track results.

Breslin calculates that if he can generate one patient from each seminar, it more than pays for the advertising.

Specialized medical seminars: snoring and sleep apnea

For people who snore or have a mate who snores, the need for a quiet solution is apparent. Sleepless nights have ruined more than one marriage. There is a growing amount of information that connects long-term physical problems with the problem of sleep apnea.

Lisa Nymark, the educational coordinator for the International Snoring Association, organizes and runs five seminars a year in the United States and Canada. The seminars try to disseminate information about various snoring problems.

Nymark attracts between 30 and 120 people to each seminar, depending on the location and timing. Participants come alone or, more often, with their partners.

"These are people who are desperate for a solution. They have often tried other techniques unsuccessfully and are willing to look at almost any option available, from specially designed anti-snoring appliances to surgery," Nymark says.

The seminar is sponsored by Integrated Health Technology, a manufacturer of an anti-snoring appliance. However, the manufacturer maintains a low profile. Its name is not mentioned at the seminar and there are no displays of its product.

An ear, nose, and throat specialist conducts the one-hour seminar. The presentation addresses the options, including the benefits and side effects of each option. The doctor's presentation is supplemented by a sleep disorder specialist who discusses lifestyle and weight loss as ways to stop snoring. The information is unbiased and objective, with no hard sell of Integrated Health Technology products.

Nymark provides a take-away handout containing support material, as well as a booklet about the International Snoring Association. Nymark finds these seminars, when handled with this level of professionalism, a powerful way to let sufferers of sleep disorders learn about their options and about the Snoring Association.

To promote the seminars, Nymark advertises on local radio and cable television stations, as well as in local newspapers.

Nonprofit organization seminars

Some nonprofit organizations that offer volunteer opportunities in developing countries, such as Canadian Crossroads International, use seminars as a recruitment tool. Crossroads does not have an advertising budget so it must count on whatever free advertising it can get. Consequently, its advertisements often get bumped, which affects audience turnout at their meetings.

Crossroads uses the seminars to walk potential volunteers through the application process and uses a slide presentation to show participants the type of work they will be doing overseas. After the presentation, there is a question-and-answer period.

Service industry seminars

If you have ever had to have your car repaired as a result of an accident, you know the uneasy feeling you have as you make your way through the maze of repair shops trying to get three quotes to present to your insurance company. For administrators responsible for the care of corporate fleets, this is a daily problem.

David and Pam Stern run Stern Auto Collision, an auto-body repair shop in Toronto. They count among their clients many fleet managers. Recognizing the confusion that sometimes surrounds vehicle repair, the Sterns ran a seminar to explain the process.

They invited 30 fleet managers to a 90-minute presentation at their shop. They took the fleet managers on a tour of the shop, with a stop at the various workstations to watch work in progress. Questions were welcome at any time during the tour.

David then took the participants into another room, where he led a 30-minute discussion clarifying what the fleet mangers had just seen. This gave the fleet managers a clearer idea of what happens to their vehicles when they are sent in for repair. There was a brief question-and-answer period and each guest received a small gift for attending.

"We don't do this regularly," Stern said. Rather, they tried it once and were so impressed with the results that they are planning to do another one this year.

Seminars in retail stores

Many retail stores strive to make their stores destinations rather than just places where customers pop in for quick purchases. Home Depot offers a series of practical seminars on various topics, with titles such as "How to Tile Your Bathroom" and "How to Make Small Electrical Repairs." Large chain bookstores such as Chapters and Barnes and Noble actively pursue authors to give short presentations about their new books or interesting ideas. A large grocery chain worked with a chef who conducted in-store demonstrations of how to cook with exotic ingredients. Some stores use in-house personnel to conduct these seminars; others bring in outsiders.

There is always an opportunity for a bright entrepreneur to approach one of these retail stores and offer to conduct the seminar for it. If your products are being sold in the store or you can tie your seminar topic to the store's products and services, you may have a match. You are limited only by the breadth of your creativity.

Before you approach the store manager, spend time walking through the store to get a feel for its customer base and for what services and products draw people into the store. With a well-thought-out plan, you will be ready to approach the store manager with your proposal.

Seminars at trade shows

Planning your seminar as part of a larger activity has many advantages. First, you can attract a larger and more targeted audience than you could if you are holding the seminar independently. Trade show operators do extensive targeted marketing for their shows. By being part of this effort, you have an opportunity to attract people who are specifically interested in the theme of the show. It also saves you the cost of marketing.

Seminars are an important trade show component. The show manager promotes your seminar as part of the overall show promotion.

If you are an exhibitor, consider an in-booth seminar. It requires reorganizing your booth layout, but I have seen seminars run successfully in a single 10-foot-by-10-foot booth. These seminars are typically ten minutes long and are packed with information. Such seminars also give you an opportunity to recruit people for a larger seminar you may be planning in the near future.

Back-of-the-room sales

Whether your seminar is intended as an immediate profit-making or lead-developing exercise, there is an additional opportunity for you to offer products for sale at the back of the room. The products you offer for sale can be yours, those from businesses you represent, or those related to your guest speaker or your sponsors. If these sales are handled correctly they can add considerable revenue to your seminar.

Back-of-the-room sales space can also be offered to a local charity. One seminar series I organize has pledged part of its revenue to the Alzheimer Society of Canada. In addition to a financial contribution, we also invite an Alzheimer representative to attend the seminar, set up a display, and promote local initiatives. The society sells revenue-producing products such as Christmas cards, T-shirts, seeds, or craft items.

Some of the products I have seen for sale at seminars include audiotapes of the presentation recorded on-site; audio-tapes by other presenters on related topics; books by the guest speaker or those related to the seminar topic; video-tape programs related to the topic or the event; newsletters and journals; resource guides listing contact names and addresses; sample forms, contracts, and checklists; bibliographies or lists of other support materials; and tip sheets.

Offering products for sale can increase your credibility whether you are the creator or distributor. However, you do want to avoid a hard sell. The participants have come to hear you or your presenter, so keep the promotion subtle and low key.

Back-of-the-room sales offer a chance to reinforce the material you presented or provide additional material which you could not cover in a brief talk. It's another opportunity for participants to get additional information so they can make an informed decision about you and your services.

Make sure to mention back-of-the-room sales in your promotional material for those people who cannot attend the seminar. Here are some tips for setting up your display:

- A pile of material dumped on a table leaves a negative impression. Proper signage is important so people know the products are for sale and not giveaways.

- Display material neatly with signage describing the benefits.

- Create a professional-looking display for your back-of-the-room sales.

- Make sure you are set up before the seminar begins and place material in a highly visible spot, such as near the refreshment table.

- Make your display look full but not overwhelming. No one likes to take the last book but if there are too many it becomes intimidating.

- Be ready to accept credit card payment as a matter of convenience as well as cash and cheques. Have receipts available.

One common way to stimulate sales is to offer a seminar special such as "we pay the tax" or "two for one," or two or three products at a discounted package price. Experiment with different packages to see what works well. Back-of-the-room sales are impulse purchases, so you want to do whatever you can to get the sale immediately. If participants have to go home to think about it, you've lost customers. Usually participants browse through the products before the seminar but wait until a break or to the end to purchase after they have had a chance to hear the speaker. They will be in a more receptive mood to buy after they have developed a rapport with you.

Another way to stimulate interest is to offer one of your products as a door prize, especially if you have the draw at the break rather than waiting to the end. This will boost early sales rather than having participants wait to see if they have won before they purchase.

Have an assistant responsible for back-of-the-room sales to keep you free to mingle with your guests. You may also consider providing an order sheet for those who can't make up their minds at the seminar.

A good rule of thumb is to assume that about 25% of your audience will buy something, so bring along enough inventory to take care of these numbers.

APPENDIX 2

RECOMMENDED READING

Axtell, Roger. *Do's and Taboos around the World*. Chicago: John Wiley and Sons, 1993.

Bender, Peter Urs. *Secrets of Power Presentations*. 2nd ed. Toronto: Achievement Group, 1991.

Drucker, Peter F. *Management: Tasks, Responsibilities, Practices*. New York: Harper and Row, 1973.

Entrepreneur Media. *Organizing and Promoting Seminars*. New York: John Wiley and Sons, 1998.

Foot, David K., and Daniel Stoffman. *Boom, Bust & Echo: How to Profit from the Coming Demographic Shift*. Toronto: Macfarlane, Walter and Ross, 1996.

Gilgrist, David. *Winning Presentations*. Aldershot, England: Gower Publishing, 1996.

Griffin, Jack. *The Do-it-Yourself Business Promotions Kit*. Englewood Cliffs, NJ: Prentice Hall, 1995.

Hurley, Brian, and Peter Birkwood. *Doing Big Business on the Internet*. 2nd ed. Vancouver: Self-Counsel Press, 1998.

Jokes, Robert. *How to Run Seminars and Workshops*. New York: John Wiley and Sons, 1993.

Karasik, Paul. *How to Make it Big in the Seminar Business*. New York: McGraw Hill, 1992.

Lambert, Clark. *Secrets of a Successful Trainer*. New York: John Wiley and Sons, 1996.

Lant, Jeffrey. *Money Talks: The Complete Guide to Creating a Profitable Workshop or Seminar in any Field*. Cambridge, MA: JLA Publications, 1997.

Malouf, Doug. *How to Create and Deliver a Dynamic Presentation.* East Roseville, Australia: Simon and Schuster, 1988.

MPI. *Meetings and Conventions: A planning guide.* Dallas: MPI, 1997.

Peoples, David. *Presentations Plus.* 2nd ed. New York: John Wiley and Sons, 1992.

Pinsky, Raleigh. *101 Ways to Promote Yourself.* New York: Avon Books, 1997.

Shenson, Howard L. *How to Develop and Promote Successful Seminars and Workshops.* New York: John Wiley and Sons, 1990.

Simerly, Robert G. *Planning and Marketing Conferences and Workshops.* San Francisco: Jossey-Bass Publishers, 1990.

Siskind, Barry. *Making Contact.* Toronto: Macmillan Canada, 1995.

___. *The Power of Exhibit Marketing.* 4th ed. Vancouver: Self-Counsel Press, 1997.